Putting Secrets

FOR THE

Weekend Golfer

Putting Secrets

FOR THE

Weekend Golfer

BY   STEVE   PAGE

ILLUSTRATIONS BY
MARY BRIDGES
AND PATRICIA SHEA

St. Martin's Griffin

NEW YORK

A THOMAS DUNNE BOOK.
An imprint of St. Martin's Press.

Illustrations by Mary Bridges and Patricia Shea

DESIGN BY JUDITH STAGNITTO ABBATE

Library of Congress Cataloging-in-Publication Data

Page, Steve (Steve B.)
    Putting secrets for the weekend golfer / by Steve
Page.
        p.   cm.
    "A Thomas Dunne book."
    ISBN 0-312-15197-7
    1. Putting (Golf)
GV979.P8P25   1997
796.352'35—dc20   96-36558
                                          CIP

First St. Martin's Griffin Edition: May 1997

10 9 8 7 6 5 4 3 2 1

To all Weekend Golfers worldwide . . .

CONTENTS

ACKNOWLEDGMENTS

Writing this book has been a challenge, a pleasure, and a reward. While it has taken several years to get this book published, I wish to thank Mary Bridges, the illustrator of all the computer-drawn illustrations in this book, for her time, patience, and incredible attention to detail. Mary deserves extra mention because she gave up many lunches and evenings to draw and revise the drawings in this book. Mary and I spent countless hours developing each illustration to the finest detail such that our readers could easily understand the point being described.

I am equally appreciative to Patricia Shea, St. Martin's illustrator, who worked with Mary's drawings to ensure that they could easily fit into a paperback format. In doing so, we made a series of changes to the drawings so they could be easily displayed and interpreted in a black and white format. Patricia was a pleasure to work with and I especially enjoyed her English accent.

I also wish to thank Marje Cates, an editor and friend, who spent many hours at home and numerous lunches helping to proofread, reason-test, and edit this book. Marje, not being a golfer, proved to be very helpful because she would question passages that did not make sense to her but seemed to make perfect sense to an avid golfer. Her editing has made this book clearer and easier to understand by the reader. From her editing and Mary's illustrations, I rewrote many passages and added illustrations to make the book readable by anyone. I can honestly say that this book is a work of art due to the diligence and patience of Mary Bridges, Marje Cates, Patricia Shea, and myself. We spent countless hours working to refine this book.

I owe many thanks to George Wieser, my agent, who believed in me and my book. He never gave up. He had tried the techniques in the book, greatly improved his putting game, and continued, relentlessly in the pursuit of a publisher. He knew it was sellable and that one day it would be published and sold all over the world. He knew that this kind of book could only be written by a golfer who had empathy for the Weekend Golfer, rather than by a golf pro who often does not fully appreciate the problems faced by average golfers. He often raised my spirits when it seemed like no one wanted to publish this unique book on the art of putting. I thank him for his patience, perseverance, and belief that this book would, one day, be published and reach the hands of hundreds of thousands, and perhaps, millions of golfers.

I owe many kind thoughts to Newell Pinch, the golfing friend who was kind enough to write a powerful foreword for this book. He spent many hours reading this book and writing a solid foreword for it, as well as, learning how to apply its techniques.

Finally, I am deeply grateful for the patience and understanding of my wife and family during those long nights and weekends while I was writing and rewriting this book with the help of Mary Bridges, Marje Cates, and Patricia Shea. Thank you.

Putting should be easy. At least it seems that way. You step up to the ball, look at the hole, and aim in the direction of the hole. Sometimes you will get close. You might even putt it in. More often than not, you'll come up short or go past the hole. You will miss 3-foot putts as often as you make them. For some, this kind of putting is okay, but for most Weekend Golfers this inconsistency is not acceptable. They want to play better, so they question their playing partners, friends, or the local golf professional. There is nothing wrong with a little guidance, but often this advice is a one-time thing and is short-lived. New problems may develop.

Once the Weekend Golfer realizes the importance of putting to his game, he or she will seek out ways to improve putting success. The author has developed with this book a solid plan for the Weekend Golfer. Simply by reading a few pages a golfer can make immediate improvements. After reading the entire book, the Weekend Golfer can become a superb putter, finding that elusive key to consistency. There is even a chapter on how to putt from off the green, something that could be useful as an alternative to chipping.

This book presents a well-organized plan for becoming a better putter almost overnight. Many tips are so simple they are often overlooked, even by some of our best putters. The book is concise, well-illustrated, and thorough in its approach.

The most important skills you will learn from this book are: the correct technique for holding a putter, addressing the ball, taking aim, stroking the ball, and sinking the putt. The next step is to STICK WITH IT.

This book is essential reading for any weekend golf enthusiast. I hope you enjoy it as much as I have.

Newell O. Pinch

Former CEO—Southern California Golf Association
Cofounder and past President—International Association of Golf Course Administrators
Former member—USGA Regional Liaison Committee

PREFACE

WHY THIS BOOK?

There are few, if any, good books written exclusively for the average Weekend Golfer, the individual who scores from 90 to 112 on a par-72 course. This book is written with the average golfer in mind, and, more specifically, on the one area of golf, *putting*, in which the average golfer can play as well as the golf pro and achieve significant score reductions. In putting, there are just a *few* basics to master and only a small number of possible lies with virtually nothing standing between the ball and the hole. With woods and irons, there are *many* swing fundamentals to master, hundreds of possible lies, and a variety of potential hazards between the ball and green.

With fewer fundamentals to learn, putting is an area the average golfer should emphasize because he can learn to become an excellent putter in a relatively short period of time. *Good putting* is the key to *good golf*—that's why putting is the main subject of this book.

Most golfing publications tend to emphasize the use of woods and irons, with putting being treated as a secondary importance. When an entire publication is devoted to putting, it's usually written in too much detail for the average golfer. While parts of the publication may be useful, it's difficult for the reader to pick and choose *which* areas will be most helpful.

This book has been designed just for the average golfer. It's a simple and easy-to-read book on putting. It has been written for *you*, the average Weekend Golfer. You are the individual who plays once per week or once or twice a month and carries a handicap of 18 to 40 on an 18-hole, par-72 course. You enjoy the game, like to score well, but seldom have time to play or practice regularly. You think about golf, watch it on television, and wish you could play more often.

A style of play is introduced that combines the successful techniques used by many golfers today and some from my own personal experiences as an average Weekend Golfer. You don't have to pick and choose. Every point discussed will help you to develop a new putting style, one to rely on and be proud of. The book advances the idea that you'll discard your current method of putting and develop a new putting style using the suggestions presented.

WHY THIS AUTHOR?

Because I'm an average Weekend Golfer like you. I am not a golf pro and never will be. While the golf pro writes a book to fit the needs of all experience levels, this book is written *for* the average Weekend Golfer authored *by* an average golfer. I have not always been a Weekend Golfer, while in college, I played daily and was a scratch golfer. I have taken hundreds of lessons.

I am also a writer. I have more than 25 years' experience in writing instructional manuals. I have down-to-earth, and sometimes unique, tips and guidelines that have worked for me and have helped improve my putting game. While my ideas are intended to help the average Weekend Golfer, any golfer can benefit.

I play about once a month and carry a 20 handicap. I hit the ball reasonably well off the tee. I'm always looking for ways to play better. It's enjoyable being outdoors, playing a game I like, with enthusiastic companions. I like to hit the ball long and straight off the tee and I'm pleased when I putt well. I try to be creative in my tactics when a difficult situation arises. I'm always thinking and analyzing. It's more fun that way.

I am normally extremely consistent when putting on the green. Being a stickler for details, I try to learn every possible aspect of putting. I have taken lessons, read many books and magazines, and studied golfing videotapes. Through much practice and patience, I discovered that consistency in putting style is the key to good golf. Using a regular putting routine, I found I could lower my golf scores simply by putting well. As I became a better putter, I found some unique but effective techniques for aiming, setting up to putt, estimating distance, and stroking the ball.

One of the more difficult parts of the game for me has been the approach shot. I have always had great difficulty getting the ball onto the green with a chip shot from as close as two feet to as far as 15 yards away from the green. I have tried repeatedly to use short irons. I was so inconsistent that I gave up on the short irons and tried running the ball onto the green using long and middle irons. Even then it was difficult to decide which iron to use depending on the lie, slope, and distance from the green. I would be short one time and long the next. It was too easy to stub the club into the ground or top the ball. I could not rely on this haphazard method for approaching the green.

Then one day, quite by accident, I tried using the putter from off the green. I was pleasantly surprised at how easy it was to control my ball from a variety of lies and distances. All I had to do was to line up as if on the green, hit the ball firmly, and it would roll onto the green nearly every time. I had better control when the ball hugged the ground while moving toward its target. I found I could get reasonably close to the flag stick from as far as 15 yards off the green. Once I was convinced that the putter was the club to use, I started to refine its usage. At first, my goal was just to get the ball onto the green. Later, as my putting abilities improved, my goal was to get within a 10-foot radius of the hole.

Putting from off the green has become a regular part of my short game. In fact, this technique has infuriated some of my friends. My success with this shot often gives me a playing advantage. My friends would never consider using a putter from off the green because *it just isn't the right club to use.* Even though they see my success, it has been hard for them to forgo that *hit like a professional, use the right club* philosophy and use a putter—they believe a golf pro would rarely use a putter from off the green—so why should they?

I can use a putter from practically any lie and distance off the green. I can putt across hard ground, over cart paths, between trees, up and down hills, through moderately heavy grass, between traps and water hazards, and even from sand bunkers. The most important thing is I can hit the ball so that it hugs the ground, while traveling relatively straight toward my intended target. I no longer have to worry about using a short or long iron where minor mistakes in the execution of the swing can result in sending the ball in any direction but the one I want.

Using a putter from off the green is not a new concept, but using it as a regular part of the approach is unique. It will become an important part of your short game once you understand why, when, where, and how to use it. And as you'll learn later, golf pros DO use the putter from off the green on more occasions than you may be aware of. Chapter 5 has been devoted to learning how to putt from off the green.

GOLF PROS DO USE THE PUTTER
FROM OFF THE GREEN

Because of my success using a putter on and from off the green, friends suggested that I write a book telling the average Weekend Golfer how to putt better. I took their advice.

Disclaimer: While it is guaranteed the average Weekend Golfer will lower his golf score of 90 or higher, this premise is based on the fact that the golfer will read and methodically apply the techniques offered in this book.

NOTES

In order to make this book easy to read, I found it necessary to make certain assumptions.

1. For discussion purposes and examples, when a golf course is referenced, it's assumed to be an 18-hole, par-72 regulation course. Unless otherwise stated, the playing conditions are considered to be nearly optimal: little wind, sunny skies, and dry fairways and greens.

2. The book is written for the right-handed golfer. The left-handed golfer should reverse the words "Right" or "Left" wherever mentioned. For example, if the passage says pick the club up with your left hand, then the left-handed golfer would pick up a club with his right hand.

3. It's assumed that the reader has an established handicap, or knows his average score so he can roughly calculate a handicap, which generally is the difference between the average score and par. Therefore, if a golfer averages 95 on a par-72 golf course, his handicap would be close to 23. Calculating handicaps can be complex and is not the subject of this book.

4. The book is written from the standpoint that the average golfer knows the meaning of commonplace golf terms like *round of golf, start time, par, bogey, handicap, short game, approach shot, penalty stroke, to hole out, fringe, lofted clubs, follow-through, flag stick*, and so forth. For these definitions, refer to a golf dictionary.

5. The term *Long Irons* refers to the 1, 2, 3 irons; *Middle Irons* to 4, 5, 6 irons; and *Short Irons* to 7, 8, 9 irons, pitching wedge, and sand wedge. A *Putter* is a putter.

6. It's assumed that the reader owns his own golf clubs, or rents a set when he arrives at the course to play or practice.

7. For simplicity in writing style, I have elected to use "he" instead of the preferred nonsexist "he or she."

8. When discussing etiquette and rules of golf, I have chosen not to differentiate between stroke and match play.

LIST OF ILLUSTRATIONS

Introduction

A NEW PUTTING STYLE IN THE MAKING

Putting style is your whole approach to putting. It's the routine you follow each time your ball position changes on or off the green. It's everything you do to get ready to putt, and finally to sink the ball. This putting style includes such details as using basic putting strategy, using a standard putter and grip, aiming and setting up to putt, judging distance, executing a smooth stroke, maintaining a positive mental attitude throughout your round, and observing proper etiquette and the rules of golf. Through the use of a standard putting style, you can become a superb putter.

NEVER UP, NEVER IN

The Weekend Golfer is rarely happy with his putting game. Typically, he will line up a putt, hit the ball in the direction of the hole, and fall short. It's atypical for him to go the full distance to the hole or past it. It goes without saying that a putt that doesn't reach the hole is never going to fall in. Many a golfer falls victim to the phrase "Never Up, Never In" because he fails to hit the ball firmly enough to reach the hole. Upon seeing his ball fall short, he expresses his emotion and goes on to the next hole as if nothing were wrong. There are conceivably millions of golfers who do the same. They haven't figured out that it's their erratic and nonstandard putting style that is keeping their scores high. They have no idea how much their putting affects their entire game. If they only knew its impact on their attitude and total game strategy, they would direct a greater percentage of their thoughts and energy to putting.

PUTTING IS OFTEN TAKEN FOR GRANTED

Learning to putt has never been foremost on the average Weekend Golfer's mind. Lee Trevino in his videotape *Putt for Dough* says, "Only two percent of all golfers have had a putting lesson." If you accept this statement as fact, it accounts for why few Weekend Golfers place putting high on their list of things to practice. Taking putting lessons has probably never occurred to them. They frequently hit hundreds of balls on a driving range with their woods and irons—but practice putting only if time permits. After all, watching a ball *fly* 150 yards in the air *is* more exciting than watching a ball *roll* 10 feet across a practice green.

The average Weekend Golfer who averages 2 to 3 putts on the green thinks that this is normal. When he thinks about improving his game, his thoughts go immediately to using his woods and irons, not to his putter. It's difficult for him to understand that putting deserves equal, if not more, attention than the woods and irons. After all, anyone can putt, right? So putting is taken for granted—because everyone is supposed to know how to putt. In many cases, the average Weekend Golfer would score better if he would concentrate more on putting than on his woods and irons.

As will be shown repeatedly throughout this book, a smooth, consistent putting stroke will not only have a positive effect on *all* aspects of your game but will help to build your confidence, which according to Ray Floyd is a key to golfing well. In his book *From 60 Yards In* he states, "Once you've a swing or a stroke that works reasonably well, your mental and emotional approach becomes 95% of the package that determines how well and how consistently you score."

Confidence in your putting can take a lot of pressure off the outcome of your shots with woods and irons. If you have a repeatable putting stroke, you'll be amazed at how easy and free your swing will become when you believe that, even if you make a mistake, you can save yourself with the putter.

PUTTING DEFINED

Putting refers to any situation in which a golfer uses a putter on a green to execute a stroke called a *putt*. While any putter can be used, the three most popular ones are the straight blade, the flange, and the mallet head. You'll find that there are hundreds of variations to these standard putters. It's your choice as to which one you want to use but you'll find that a standard putter often works best as you develop your new putting style.

A putt is normally the final stroke on a hole—unless you sink the ball from off the green. While you can take many putts before sinking the ball into the hole, par golf allows for 2 putts on each green, or a total of 36 putts per round on an 18-hole golf course. Shots executed from off the green with a putter are counted as approach shots, not putts. Your final golf score is comprised of all strokes taken on or off the green with any club, including any penalty strokes incurred.

PERSONAL PUTTING GOALS

In order of priority, there are three personal putting goals: good, great, and superb. You should strive first to become *good*, then *great*, and finally *superb*.

1. *Good putting* is par golf which means that you will average 2 putts per hole with your total putting score not exceeding 36 putts per round.

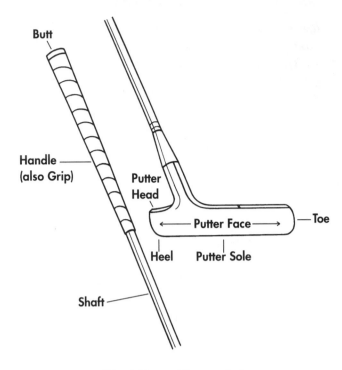

Fig. 1 Putter Characteristics

2. *Great putting* means that your total putting score will not exceed 32 to 33 putts per round.

3. *Superb putting* means that your total putting score will not exceed 28 to 30 putts per round. This would be pro status. This is your final objective. When you're able to achieve 28 to 30 putting strokes per round, you'll be doing exceptionally well and can expect a significant score reduction.

According to Dave Pelz, in his book *Putt Like the Pros*, "Putting represents 43 percent of all shots played. All your iron shots combined equal only about one-third the number of strokes taken with the putter. (That should really make you think about where to devote your practice time. Most golfers practice iron shots more than anything else.)" He adds, "Based on this definition, the 43 percent value of putting holds up very well for all golfers except those who score over 100. The professional who shoots 70 will average about 30 strokes with the putter; most 85 shooters will use the putter around 35 times; and the 95 shooter will putt around 38 times per round."

For simplicity's sake, it's my recommendation that you apply Pelz's 43 percent rule to any score. For instance, if your average score is 105, your putting strokes should total about 45 times per round. Or if your average score is 112, your putting strokes should total around 48 times per round. Try it with your average score. No matter how many putts you take, start keeping a record of your golf scores. Separate your putting score from your total score so you can make a realistic comparison in six months and measure your overall improvement.

Applying Pelz's logic to the third objective of becoming a *superb putter* and achieving a putting score of 28 to 30, the Weekend Golfer who normally shoots 112 with 48 putts can lower his total score to 94 by lowering his putting score from 48 to 30. This translates to a score reduction of 18. Subtracting 18 from 112 results in a net score of 94. Similarly, the Weekend Golfer who shoots 95 can lower his total score to 87 by lowering his putting score from 38 to 30. This is a score reduction of 8. Subtracting 8 from 95 results in a net score of 87.

Putting is not really difficult.

> **THE AVERAGE WEEKEND GOLFER FREQUENTLY MAKES THE SAME MISTAKE ON THE GREEN OVER AND OVER AGAIN BECAUSE HE DOESN'T KNOW ANY BETTER.**

He hasn't been taught to maintain a consistent putting style. Putting is a skill that can be readily learned through practice and patience. Stroking a putter is relatively easy. It requires a short backstroke and a short forward stroke. There is no body turn. The putterhead stays low to the ground. The ball is on top of the grass. The target, usually the hole, is nearly always visible with no hazards in the way. The only thing you have to do is to get that tiny little ball into a hole which is about 2½ times wider than the ball. The simplicity of the putting stroke makes it possible for the average Weekend Golfer to putt as well as the golf pro. The goal of becoming a *superb putter* is achievable. Read on and find out how.

CHAPTER 1

Planning, Visualizing, and Playing Realistically

A TYPICAL DAY OF GOLF

On the day you plan to play golf, you'll wake up eager to get to the course. Assuming you have a start time, you'll plan to arrive at the course about one hour before tee-off time. Upon arrival, you may recheck the tee-off time with the starter. You'll probably sit and have something to eat or drink, chat with some friends, or browse in the golf shop. Eventually, you may get a bucket of balls and go out to the driving range, if there is one. You'll use up your balls hitting woods and irons one after another, as far and as straight as possible toward the range targets. Time permitting, you may practice for a while on the putting green. You're now ready to play.

When called to check in, you report to the starter, pay the golf fees, rent either a pull cart or a powered golf cart (you rarely walk and carry your own clubs), pick up a score card and pencil, and go to the first tee to join the rest of your assigned group. Typically, the first hole on an 18-hole golf course is a par 4 or par 5. When it's your turn, you usually select your driver and try to hit the ball as far as possible. You walk or drive to your ball. You figure out how far you are from the green, select another club, and again hit the ball as far as possible. But if your ball lies 180 to 250 yards from the green, you will wait for the golfers ahead to finish their play and leave the green. You then hit your ball toward the green. Usually, however, you'll be way short or off to the left or right of the green. Rarely does the ball land on the green.

You continue to play your ball until it reaches the green. You then pick up your putter, walk up to your ball, wait your turn, step up to the ball, take quick aim, and hit the ball toward the hole. After finally sinking one of your putts, you'll pick up your ball, wait for the others in your group to hole out, walk off the green, put away your putter, and take out the score card. You mentally recount the number of strokes and write that total for the first hole. You continue to play the remaining holes in a similar manner. You finish with an average round. You may score above average once in a while, but, most of the time, your score is average or worse.

WHY DIDN'T YOU SCORE WELL?

Because—you failed to plan your day. You didn't allow sufficient practice time before starting your round and you probably didn't practice correctly either. You just hit balls randomly on the driving range. You didn't plan any of your shots. You tried to hit every shot long and straight like a pro. When on the green, you didn't stick to a particular putting style or game plan. You didn't think creatively or analyze your shots. Not knowing any better, you just accepted everything that happened.

PLANNING YOUR DAY TO MAKE THINGS GO RIGHT

If your day lacks strategy, then typically so does your game. If you plan your day before arriving at the golf course and before starting your round of play, it will greatly influence your overall game. If you determine how much practice time you need on the driving range, on the putting green, and how much time you'll need for any other activities before tee-off, you can estimate the best time to arrive at the course.

For example, if you have a starting time of 10:00 A.M. and think you need about 20 minutes on the driving range, about 10 minutes on the putting green, and 40 minutes of relaxation before your tee-off time, you should arrive at the golf course at least 70 minutes prior to tee-off, or around 8:50 A.M. This kind of planning will give you a relaxed, unrushed start that can only help your mental attitude toward your game.

By the time you check in, you should already be thinking about your round of golf. When driving up to the course, you should note its condition and layout as well as green size, pin placement, fairway width, and location of water hazards and sand bunkers. Once at the course, you should ask the starter if there are yardage markers on the course. He can tell you how to identify the markers (palm trees, concrete slabs, etc.). He may offer to sell you a yardage map. Buy one—it can be very helpful.

STRATEGY ON THE COURSE

When you're ready to hit from the first tee box, mentally plan each shot from tee to green *before* lifting a club. This planning is important to your entire game. If you hit a shot without thought as to where it may land, the next shot could be even more difficult than the first. Randomly hitting shot after shot will almost always result in trouble with each and every stroke. You must look carefully at what confronts you and select a target. You must plan each shot all the way to the green and have several shots in mind when you're ready to approach the green. "You have to stroke and analyze, stroke and analyze"—a quote from Arnold Palmer's *Complete Book of Putting*. You must visualize each shot, play realistically, and play the percentage shot whenever possible.

1. VISUALIZE EACH SHOT. Consider fairway width and length, trees, out-of-bounds stakes, hazards, distance, and lie before selecting and using a club. Evaluate the risks of each potential landing position.

Visualize the ball's trajectory and its landing somewhere in your target zone. Ray Floyd, in *From 60 Yards In*, emphasizes this thinking and says, "The player can induce a preview, a visualization, of a shot. The mind does control the body, and if you work hard at controlling your mind, using it in the right way, you can produce the proper response from your muscles. If you concentrate, you can see the putt rolling into the hole, see the pitch shot floating high over the bunker, and setting close to the hole."

This thought process applies to both fairway and approach shots. The strategy is not only helpful for staying out of trouble but will be important to all shots from tee box to green. Plan carefully and completely. Keep your eyes and mind open while constantly looking for opportunities to save strokes. Positive planning will help you to maintain a winning mental attitude that will help to give you a feeling of assurance when preparing to hit a ball.

2. BE REALISTIC. The golf pro will consistently hit the green in regulation (par), but you're an average golfer and don't have his control or power. You can't expect to hit like a pro. You can play golf for years without coming to this realization. But once you do, your game will improve immediately. So play your own game. With realistic goals, what may be only an average shot for the pro may be a good one for you.

PLAY WITHIN YOUR CAPABILITIES AND PLAY TO YOUR HANDICAP.

When you're lying 180 to 250 yards from the green, don't expect to hit the ball that full distance. In the majority of cases, you can't execute a perfect, long, and straight shot to the green. You may feel confident that you can reach the green, but you're not playing to your handicap and you're holding up play for those behind you. Take that club you're comfortable with, lay the ball up short, and be ready to make it to the green on the next shot.

If you normally shoot one over par on each hole (18-handicap), play that way. Always trying to reach the green in regulation will result in inconsistent golf. If you use the shots you're best at and reach the green in three shots instead of two on a par-4 hole, you're more likely to bogey the hole than to make par. Going for two perfectly executed shots on a hole to reach a green in regulation can only lead to trouble and frustration. You might get behind a tree, land in a fairway bunker or water hazard, or even go out-of-bounds if you're constantly trying to make one brilliant shot after another. This effort will cause more shots, not fewer, to be taken. You must be realistic and only play those shots you're good at. As Gary Player from *Golf Begins at 50* puts it, "Learn to play your shot, not someone else's. If you know you should lay up short of a water hazard, ignore the fact that others are trying to carry it. Stick to your guns and lay up. Often, you'll have the last laugh."

3. PLAY THE PERCENTAGE SHOT. The main difference between you and the golf pro is that he knows and uses his strengths while avoiding his weaknesses. He plays the shot that gives him the best chance of success. He plays the percentage shot. You, too, can play the percentage shot. Taking a percentage shot means selecting and using a club that you're comfortable with—one with which you are fairly certain you can hit a ball a specific distance and in a particular direction every time.

For example, if you rarely hit the 4-iron 165 yards but consistently hit your 5-iron 145 yards relatively straight and you are lying 160 yards from the green, the percentage shot is to use the 5-iron and play a second shot onto the green from 15 yards out. If you select the 4-iron, you'll be playing against the odds and praying that this will be **the** time that you hit it the full 160 yards straight at the green.

Playing the percentage shot can reduce high scores. You can't expect to play your best golf if you hit unrealistic, low-percentage shots. There will be times when you'll be playing competitively and the low-percentage shot will be necessary to take the lead. Be cautious. Prepare yourself for that shot and be ready to accept the consequences both in terms of your score and emotions. As you become proficient with your putter, you'll even start using the putter as a percentage shot from off the green.

If you continually try to hit one brilliant shot after another, rather than the percentage shot, you'll hit a few good shots, but for the most part you'll be erratic and inconsistent. This can only lead to frustration and a loss of self-control.

Blowups from a bad temper probably have ruined as many golf games as mishit shots. The problem of dealing with a bad temper on the golf course can be the subject of an entire book. So if you hit a bad shot, step back and count to ten. Accept the bad shot as gracefully as possible, which is easier said than done, and rearrange your plans to make up for it. Keep in mind what Jack Nicklaus said in his book *Jack Nicklaus' Playing Lessons,* "You have to whip yourself before you can whip the course." Which means, you must control your temper before you can start scoring well. An even temper can help instill confidence in your game, an attitude that can only help your total score.

CHAPTER 2

Finding the Correct
Line of Putt

PLANNING STARTS YOU OFF RIGHT

Determining the line of putt starts well before you reach the green. Think about possible putting situations when planning your approach shot. Where you land that shot makes the crucial difference in the number of strokes taken around or on the green. The size, shape, and even the texture of the green can determine where you want your ball to land. The closer you can place your approach shot to the flag stick, the fewer putts you'll need to take.

Finding the correct line of putt is one of the first steps in developing a putting style. You'll learn what it takes to establish an accurate line of putt. Slope, grain, grass height and type, dampness of green, and ground conditions of the green are the key variables that the average Weekend Golfer should consider when calculating a line of putt. As you'll quickly learn, if you only consider slope in your calculations, your putting will improve immediately. It's when you start using the other variables to your advantage that you'll be on the road to becoming a superb putter.

LINE OF PUTT DEFINED

The line of putt is an invisible line from ball to hole—the line along which the ball must travel to reach and fall into the hole. According the *USGA's Rules of Golf,* "This is the line that the player wishes his ball to take after a stroke on the putting green. It includes a reasonable distance on either side of the intended line but the line doesn't extend beyond the hole."

The position of the ball on the green becomes the beginning of the line; the hole is the end of the line.

In reality, of course, this invisible line is not a line—it's more like a channel with boundaries within which the ball must travel. Look at the definition again. It says that ". . . it includes a reasonable distance on either side of the intended line. . . ."

With the hole being 4.25 inches in diameter and the regulation ball having a diameter of 1.68 inches, the ball doesn't have to follow a fine line to reach the hole, nor does it have to hit the dead center of the hole to go in. Normally, if just half the ball hits the hole, it will fall in. This adds another 0.84 inches of "drop" area to each side of the hole, making the hole appear about 3½ times as wide as the ball.

All of a sudden, the hole becomes a much larger target. With this seemingly larger hole at the end of the line of putt, the ball can waver a little off line (staying within the channel) and still have a chance of dropping into the hole should at least half of the ball touch the edge of the hole.

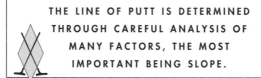

THE LINE OF PUTT IS DETERMINED
THROUGH CAREFUL ANALYSIS OF
MANY FACTORS, THE MOST
IMPORTANT BEING SLOPE.

The other factors play a lesser role but still should be understood and applied when calculating this line. *If slope is not considered,* putting becomes a matter of luck. According to *Webster's Tenth New Collegiate Dictionary,* slope is defined as an "upward or downward slant or incli-

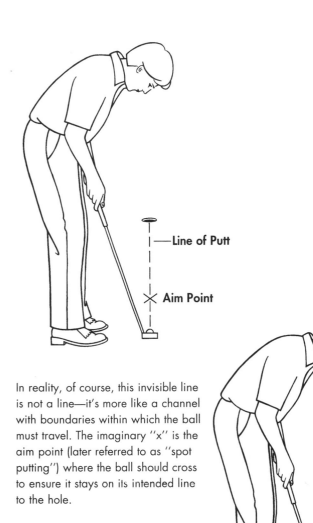

—Line of Putt

Aim Point

In reality, of course, this invisible line is not a line—it's more like a channel with boundaries within which the ball must travel. The imaginary "x" is the aim point (later referred to as "spot putting") where the ball should cross to ensure it stays on its intended line to the hole.

Channel

Figure 2. Line of Putt

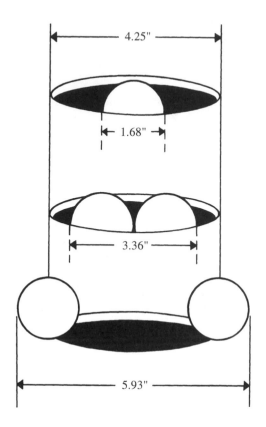

Figure 3. Hole Size Appears 3½ Times as Wide as the Ball

nation." In golfing terms, it means the slant of the green. Slope is important because it's the critical factor that determines if your line of putt is right-to-left or left-to-right breaking, or has no break at all.

If you hit a ball toward a hole without considering slope, you'll get close only if there is a little break and if you've hit it hard enough to reach the vicinity of the hole. If the ball is not hit hard enough or does not go in the right direction, it will fall short or break away from the hole and may end up farther away than when you started.

SLOPE DETERMINATION

When calculating slope, you must first survey your line of putt from all angles. This will give you a quick visual as to whether the ground between the ball and the hole is uphill, downhill, or flat. Next, you must determine whether the ground between your ball and the hole slants to the left or to the right, or is flat. To accomplish this you must first find the *baseline*—the line that you'll use to measure the height of your break, or *break point*. Put another way, the break point is the highest point along a line of putt. It's the point where the ball will start to break into the hole. You'll learn in the next few sections how to find the break point.

Once you have identified the baseline and break point, you'll be able to determine a fairly accurate line of putt which starts from the position of your ball, rises up to the break point (if there is one), and curves down to the hole. Given the proper ball speed, you'll be able to roll the ball along your line of putt, over this break point wherever it may be, and down into the hole.

*FINDING THE BASELINE

Finding the baseline is easy. Start by standing behind your ball. Look at the hole and visualize an imaginary line extending straight from the center of the hole back to your ball. This is the baseline; the line on which all your putts are based.

PLUMB-BOBBING: THE METHOD FOR FINDING THE BREAK POINT ON A LINE OF PUTT

The break point is determined by using an aiming method called *plumb-bobbing*. With this method, aiming becomes relatively easy. Your ball will get much closer to the hole and you'll be pleased with the results. Scientifically, plumb-bobbing is a very accurate system of determining the slant of the green. It'll show you which side of the baseline your ball will break. You'll then be able to determine if the

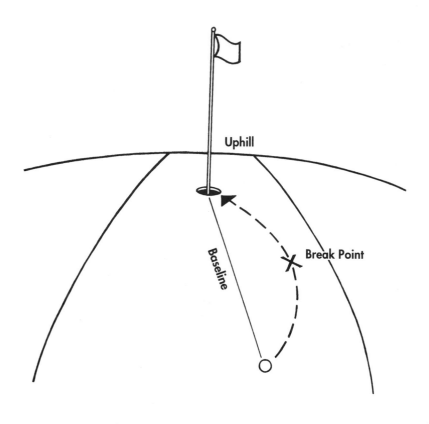

Figure 4. Slope Characteristics

putt breaks right-to-left, left-to-right, or has no break at all. It'll also show you approximately how much of a break the ball will need to reach and drop into the hole. In the case of a right-to-left breaking putt, the break point will be to the right of the baseline. In the case of a left-to-right breaking putt, the break point will be to the left of the baseline. You'll learn later how to determine placement of an imaginary "X" (spot putting) to ensure your ball travels on its intended line.

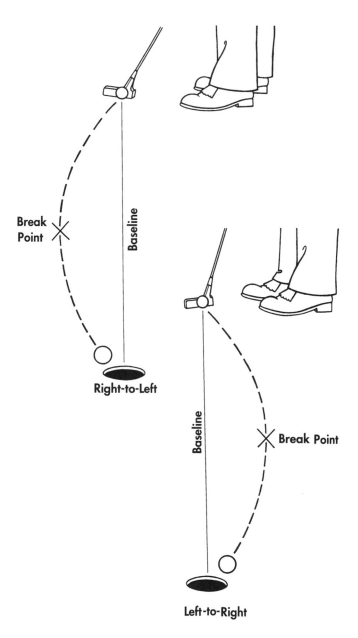

Figure 5. Breaking Putts

While plumb-bobbing is used by many golf pros, it's rarely used by the average golfer. I'm not sure why but I can only guess that it's a lack of understanding its use. Perhaps the average golfers tried it a few times, were unsuccessful, and didn't try again—or maybe they regarded it as just another gimmick.

PLUMB-BOBBING IS NEITHER A GIMMICK NOR AS COMPLICATED AS IT SOUNDS

Plumb-bobbing is relatively easy to learn but difficult to put into writing. It's rather like telling a visitor from another planet how to tie a shoelace. With some study, practice, and success, you'll get the idea.

When plumb-bobbing, you'll actually be able to see the slant of the green and you'll be able to visualize the break point. The first step to learning the art of plumb-bobbing is to figure out which eye is the dominant one. If you use the wrong eye, plumb-bobbing will never work. The *Golf Magazine's Handbook of Golf Strategy* has an excellent method for determining which eye is dominant. Try it. It works. Remember you must know which eye is dominant for this aiming method to work.

According to *Webster's Tenth New Collegiate Dictionary*, a plumb line is defined as, "a line (as of cord) that has at one end a weight (as a plumb bob) and is used especially to determine verticality." Relating this concept to golf, the putter shaft becomes the plumb line and the putterhead becomes the plumb bob.

By determining the verticality of the ground where you stand, you'll easily be able to visualize ground slant, if there is any.

PLUMB-BOBBING REVEALS HILLS, BUMPS, AND OTHER UNDULATIONS BETWEEN YOUR BALL AND THE HOLE.

For the straight putt (the putt with no break), the break point is directly on the baseline.

Figure 6. Straight Putt—No Break Point

With the naked eye, you'd only be guessing. With plumb-bobbing, the average Weekend Golfer stands a good chance of establishing a very accurate line of putt.

Plumb-bobbing is often recommended by golf pros for use on courses in the mountains or by the sea. On mountain courses in particular, optical illusions can affect your game. The green may seem perfectly level when you're standing on it, but actually it will nearly always be sloping away from the nearest mountain. Similarly, greens by the sea nearly always slant toward the sea.

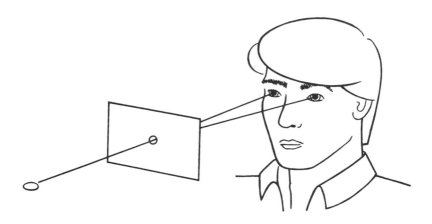

"Take a normal-sized sheet of paper and cut a hole in the center. Place a penny on the floor. While holding the paper at arm's length with both hands, look at the penny through the hole with both eyes open, then alternately close each eye. The eye that can still see the penny is the dominant eye. Usually, the right eye is the dominant eye for the right-handed person."

Figure 7. Finding the Dominant Eye

1. HOW DO YOU PLUMB-BOB?   Stand approximately four to five feet behind your ball and find the baseline—the line extending from the hole back to the ball. (On shorter putts, reduce the distance to two or three feet.) Facing the hole, straddle this line. Position your feet at shoulder's width apart. Be sure your stance is centered directly over the baseline. Squat down. You can remain standing but you will have to experiment with both the squatting and standing positions.

Grasp the putter handle near the bottom of the grip area or where it's comfortable. Hold the putter at arm's length between your thumb and forefinger, with your right hand if your right eye is the dominant one. Raise or lower the putter so that the center of the grip is level with your eyes. Maintain a light grip and let the shaft hang freely. Do not tighten your grip. The putter toe should face the hole. Hold the putter so that the lower part of the shaft bisects the ball. Run your dominant eye up the shaft and sight the putt. Note the relationship

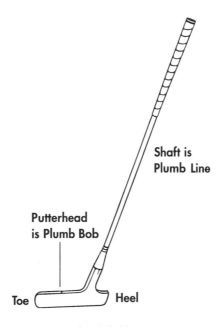

Shaft is
Plumb Line

Putterhead
is Plumb Bob

Toe   Heel

Figure 8. Plumb-bobbing Components

of the putter shaft to the hole. This is the maximum height the ball must rise before turning toward the hole. This is the break point. Don't confuse the break point with the imaginary "X" used in spot putting. You'll learn more about spot putting in Chapter 4.

Unless the putt is straight, the hole will become visible either to the left or right of the putter shaft. If the hole appears to be to the left of the shaft, the ground slopes right-to-left. If the hole is appears to be to the right of the shaft, the ground slopes left-to-right. If the shaft covers the hole, there is no break and you've got a straight putt. The exact location of the break point is dependent on the speed of the ball. Plumb-bobbing does work! You may have to experiment with the instructions. Once you learn it, you'll always use it to help you determine the break on a line of putt.

As your putting improves, you'll be able to sight the break, like golf pros do, without plumb-bobbing. You can then reserve its use for severe slopes or when playing a course in the mountains or by the sea where the greens will play optical illusion on you.

2. IS PLUMB-BOBBING FLAWLESS? False readings can be caused by such factors as multiple slopes, ball speed, wet greens, or putter type. Each of these situations is addressed below:

A. Multiple Slopes. Plumb-bobbing works best on putts where the slope is constant from ball to hole. It's most accurate on putts up to 20 feet in length. As you move farther out, there's a greater chance that the slope where you're standing and the slope around the hole will be different, which could result in an inaccurate reading of the slope.

Reading a putt that crosses over several slopes is difficult even for the golf pro. For the time being, don't worry about any slope other than the one on which the hole is located. Just putt as if there is only one slope. When your putting ability improves, you'll be able to use the plumb-bobbing basics to read a multiple-breaking putt.

B. Ball Speed. Different ball speeds can change your line of putt. Except for the straight putt, there will never be a single correct line of putt because different ball speeds require different lines of putt on the same slope. Depending on how hard you like to hit the ball, you may have to lower the height of the break point for a faster ball or raise it for a slower one.

C. Wet Greens. When the greens are wet, putts will not break as much as perceived. You'll probably have to reduce your estimated break point by at least half the perceived distance.

D. Putter Type. Don't expect to plumb-bob with an odd-shaped or unevenly balanced putter. The putter should be fairly evenly weighted on both sides of the shaft to give you the best chance of determining an accurate line of putt. You can try plumb-bobbing with any putter but it will not be effective if the putter is not well balanced.

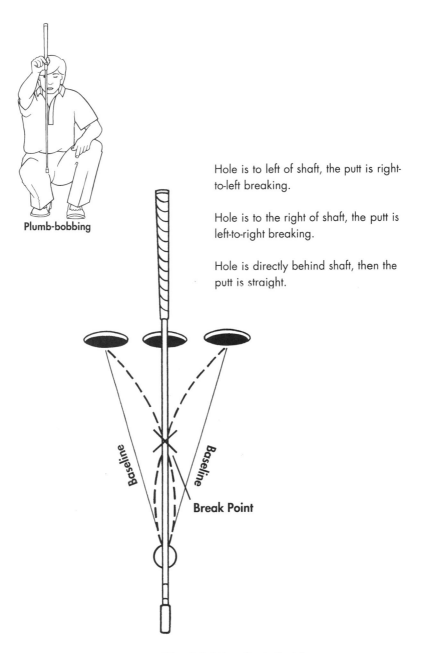

Plumb-bobbing

Hole is to left of shaft, the putt is right-to-left breaking.

Hole is to the right of shaft, the putt is left-to-right breaking.

Hole is directly behind shaft, then the putt is straight.

Baseline

Baseline

Break Point

Figure 9. Plumb-bobbing Basic Position

Plumb-bobbing is my preferred method for judging break—it has rarely led me astray. Why aim with the eye when accuracy is readily achievable with plumb-bobbing. I may hit the ball too hard or too gently but when I step back and reevaluate my original line of putt, I usually find that it was quite accurate—I just didn't stroke the ball at the right speed.

GRAIN — AND ITS IMPORTANCE

Next to slope, grain is the most important variable to be considered when determining the line of putt. Almost every publication I studied while researching this book mentioned grain. Each author explained the importance of grain and used a variety of illustrations, but even with good illustrations, I found the concept of grain confusing and felt that the average Weekend Golfer needed a simple explanation.

> **GRAIN IS NOTHING MORE THAN THE PREVAILING DIRECTION IN WHICH THE GRASS BLADES ARE GROWING.**

Even that was a mouthful! Unfortunately, grain is important to us because it affects the roll of a ball across the surface of the green. Once you understand the importance of grain and start applying that understanding to your line of putt calculations, you'll see noticeable improvement in your putting. It is not essential that you understand grain, but that understanding will certainly help you become a better putter.

1. THE EFFECT OF GRAIN ON PUTTS. The direction in which grass grows (grain) as well as its thickness and height will have varying effects on a putt. To become a better putter, you must understand how grain affects your ball. Putts will roll faster and farther, gliding easily across the top of the grass, when the grass blades are turned away from the ball. This is called *with the grain* or *downgrain*. Putts

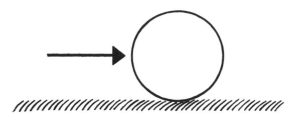

Figure 10. With the Grain

roll slower when the grass blades are turned toward the ball. The ball butts up against the grass causing it to quickly slow down. This is called *against the grain* or *upgrain.* Putts which must roll diagonally across the grass blades will normally break in the direction the grass is growing. This is called *cross-grain.*

2. A SIMPLE WAY TO FIND GRAIN DIRECTION. As I have stated, grain is difficult to explain. Where grain is concerned, experience is definitely the best teacher. If the lawn mower has been hard at work, it's very difficult to determine the direction of grain. One neat trick is to stand somewhere behind your ball, while looking at the hole, and notice whether the green surface has a shiny or dull appearance. Read on and see why.

A. With the Grain. If you see a shine (surface appears light or silvery), it means that the grass is growing away from you and you'll be putting with the grain. In such a case, your ball will travel farther with less effort on your part.

B. Against the Grain. If you see little or no shine (surface appears dark, dirty, or dull), it means you will be putting against the grain and you must use an extra firm stroke to make your ball reach the hole.

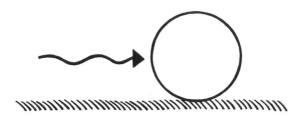

Figure 11. Against the Grain

C. Cross-grain. If the surface in front of you appears to have a combination of shine, and no shine, it probably means that you'll be putting across the grain. It's difficult enough to understand any grain definition, let alone cross-grain—so if you have trouble with the concept of grain, don't worry about it until you've made significant improvement in your putting game. Just treat cross-grain putts like straight ones for the time being.

Sometimes the weather or even the time of day can make it difficult to decide whether there *is* a shine on the green's surface. So whether its cloudy or late in the day, look at the way the grass grows around the hole and you may find a clue as to grain direction. Grass will lie across the edge of the hole in the direction it's growing. If the grass is overhanging the front edge of the hole (and away from you), you'll be putting with the grain. Conversely, if the grass is growing away from the front edge (and toward you), you'll be putting against the grain.

Another trick to understanding the differences in shine is to find a thick carpet and try some experiments. If you brush down the carpet nap, the carpet will appear bright and shiny (with the grain). If you brush against the nap, the carpet will appear dark and less shiny (against the grain). If you brush across the nap, one side will appear shinier than the other (cross-grain). With practice, you'll learn how to translate these experiments into reading grain on the course.

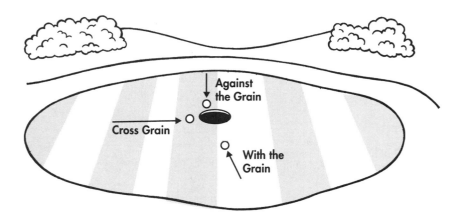

Figure 12. Cross-grain

3. STILL DON'T UNDERSTAND GRAIN? Forget about it for a while. Just concentrate on learning to read slopes. With a good understanding of slope, you'll be able to ignore the other variables until you have developed your new putting style and are showing a significant improvement in your putting game. Reading grain will become easier as you become a better putter. After you've developed your new putting style, you can reread this chapter. It will make a lot more sense when you've practiced and fine-tuned your putting style.

Some golfers argue that break and grain are not important considerations if you're a bold hitter. They say, *"Just hit the ball firmly and drive your ball through the break and grain, toward the hole."* While this may be true, your whole putting style then becomes a matter of feel. Experiment for yourself and decide whether you want to learn the mechanics of putting and apply them scientifically or if you want to base your putting techniques on feel and luck alone.

GRASS HEIGHT

If the grass has just been mowed, the ball will roll faster than when the grass blades are long. An uncut green played early in the morning can be very slow and can require a much harder stroke than in the afternoon, when the sun has dried things off, or when the lawn mower has been hard at work, or when players have been tromping all over the green.

DAMP OR WET GRASS

A damp or wet green can cause your putt to break less than the apparent slope indicates. Whether there is a light or heavy covering of water, the greens will be slower and the ball will not roll as far, or break as much, as on dry greens when you use a normal stroke. You have to stroke the ball more firmly than normal. With time and practice, you'll learn the best way to play under wet conditions.

Dave Pelz, author of *Putt Like the Pros*, gives a tip for playing in the rain: "When you mark your ball, remove it from the surface and dry it carefully. Then replace it gently so only the small part of the ball touching the green gets wet. Concentrate on stroking the ball as squarely as possible on the line you intend, with no sidespin. If you can do this, as the ball rolls along, only the center will get wet. This makes the ball heavier around the center, and it will roll straight and truer (a gyroscopic effect). Remember to play for less break, keep your stroke firm, and use wetness to your advantage."

GRASS TYPES

If you're a studious golfer and want to know as much as possible about green conditions, knowledge of grass types used on the greens can be helpful in finding grain and establishing your line of putt. But for most golfers, knowing the type of grass won't mean much. I have noted below the basic characteristics of two very common grass types used on golf courses, namely, Bermuda and Bent grass.

1. BERMUDA GRASS. Bermuda grass is used extensively in the South, Southwest, Caribbean area, and Southern California because it grows well in hot climates. The grass is very grainy, wiry, bristly, and stubby to the touch. This makes for a coarse putting surface. It's difficult to see the grain of Bermuda grass when simply looking at the blades. If you remember nothing else, remember the key characteristic to Bermuda grass is that it grows toward the setting sun, east to west.

Jack Nicklaus says that knowledge of Bermuda grass will give you an idea of how to putt on it. In his book *Jack Nicklaus' Lesson Tee,* he says, "I try in putting to catch the ball slightly on the upstroke. This type of stroke gets the ball rolling truly end over end faster and better than a downward motion of the putterhead. Also, by hitting slightly upward, I guard against catching the grass before the ball, which on Bermuda will always decelerate the putterhead and twist it off-line."

2. BENT GRASS. Bent grass is widely used in the United States— along both seacoasts, in the North, Northeast, and Midwest. It grows toward mountains and away from water. Bent grass is naturally short-bladed and has very little grain. Generally, Bent grasses provide a slick, smooth putting surface when closely mowed. If you're playing on bent grasses which are difficult to read, it is safe to assume that the grass is growing in the direction of the drainage, toward the low side of the green, or toward the nearest low-lying land.

INSPECTING THE GROUND CONDITIONS ALONG A LINE OF PUTT

After determining your line of putt by analysis of slope, grain, grass height and type, and dampness of green, carefully inspect the proposed line of putt and pick up any impediments which could affect the roll of the ball. Be careful not to touch the line of putt—penalty strokes can be incurred by doing so.

According to the *USGA's Rules of Golf in Pictures,* the line of putt must not be touched *except* you may:

1.   Move sand and loose soil on the green and other loose impediments (defined as natural objects such as stones, leaves, twigs, branches, and the like, dung, worms, insects and casts or heaps made by them, provided they are not fixed or growing, and are not solidly embedded and do not adhere to the ball) by picking them up or by brushing them aside with your hand or a club, without pressing anything down (causal water cannot be brushed aside). Dew and frost are not loose impediments;

2.   Place the putterhead in front of the ball without pressing anything down;

3.   Press down a ball marker;

4.   Lift the ball when marking or cleaning it;

5.   Measure the distance between the ball and the hole;

6.   Repair old hole plugs or ball marks (spike marks, cup imperfections, and other damage to the green's surface cannot be repaired until everyone has completed the hole); and

7.   Remove movable obstructions.

FINAL LINE OF PUTT

The final line of putt refers to the imaginary line, or channel, calculated using the techniques covered in this chapter. I selected slope as being the most important variable in this calculation. In many cases, depending on your putting abilities, you may look for grain or grass type first. You have to be the judge as to which variables you'll consider for your putts. But to begin, I am recommending that slope determination be your first and foremost concern. When your putting style improves, you can refine your calculations and add the effects of the other variables.

   The line of putt is only final in the sense that you intend to make the putt. If you take several strokes to get into the hole, then each time your ball position changes, you need to establish a new line. This applies to putts of all lengths. Too many golfers will carefully line up long putts and then fail to use the same procedure on short ones. I suppose they conclude that the short line of putt is straight and that a hard stroke will send the ball into the center of the hole. Since truly straight putts are rare, experience shows that even the short putt requires the same, if not, more concentration than the long putt.

1. DON'T RUSH YOUR PUTTS. Have you ever hit a 50-foot putt, missed it by 2 feet, stepped up to the ball and said, "Let me finish my putt while I'm hot?" This action was just the opposite of what you should have done. In essence you were saying, "I don't understand why I missed the first putt, but let me continue while my momentum and confidence are high. If I stop now and wait my turn, the pressure will increase, making the short putt more difficult." You didn't do yourself a favor. In such a case, you should either wait your turn (to slow down your pace) or step back and reevaluate your new line of putt. This will help to reestablish your confidence level. If you step up to the putt without thinking, not only will your normal putting style be compromised but you will be trying to force the ball into the hole without taking aim while running the risk of missing the putt.

2. DON'T CHANGE YOUR MIND AT THE LAST MINUTE. Once you've selected your final line of putt and have established firmly in your mind the direction and speed necessary to get close to or into the hole, *don't change your mind* in midstream. If you have any doubt at the last minute just before you take your backstroke, *stop everything.* Step back. Reevaluate what you're about to do. Look at the putt as if it were from a new ball position. I realize this is difficult and you may think it's a waste of time, but you *must* proceed slowly and carefully. It will pay off. This strategy can come into play throughout your game. For instance, if you're about to take your backswing with your driver and someone talks or sneezes, it's best if you can stop, relax, take a deep breath, and start your routine of setting up all over again.

CHAPTER 3

Setting Up to Putt

A SETUP YOU CAN RELY ON

Some professional golfers have said that it doesn't make any difference how you set up to putt. I believe they mean it doesn't make any difference as long as your setup is consistent from one time to the next. To maintain that consistency, you must establish standards you can rely on. The way you set up to swing a baseball bat, serve a tennis ball, punt a football, or shoot a basketball should be executed in the same way every time. If you change your setup from one time to the next, the results will be unpredictable. Watch the golf pros. You'll find that their setup is the same every time.

You've already learned how to establish a line of putt. Now learn how to position yourself in relation to that line. This is a standard putting setup based on the successful techniques of many golfing professionals and on techniques I have found useful on my road to becoming a superb putter. The way you set up generally involves your body position, club position, and the type of putter you use. You'll learn how to stand, grip the putter, position the putterhead, align the ball, and to select the correct putter to use. With some concentrated practice on the putting green, you'll find that this change in the way you set up to putt will have a significant impact on the number of putts you take. You'll now be able to aim correctly, set up properly, and hit the ball solidly every time. This new putting style will greatly boost your confidence, reduce tension, and generally improve your game.

BODY POSITION

How you stand, position your head and eyes, grip the putter, and hold your hands are the first concerns to setting up your putt.

1. STANCE. The way you stand when putting involves positioning your feet and aligning your body in relation to the ball and the line of putt along which you want the ball to move. The key to a good stance is stability and balance.

Position yourself over the ball. Stand tall and lean over from your hips just slightly. Place your feet about shoulder's width apart so that you feel balanced in a state of relaxed readiness. Make sure the toes of both feet are on an imaginary line parallel to the line of putt. Put your weight on the insides of your feet for a more solid position and flex your knees a bit to reduce tension. Crouch over the ball so that your stance becomes secure and allows you to stroke the ball solidly. Keep your eyes directly over the ball. Tuck your elbows into your sides and rest your right elbow very gently on your right hipbone. Square your shoulders so that they are parallel to the line of putt. How far you bend over from your hips is a matter of personal preference as long as you keep your eyes over the ball and the putter sole flat on the green.

To check the solidity of your stance, have a friend give you a little shove. If you waver, recheck your stance for stability and balance. The ideal stance ensures your shoulders, arms, hips, and feet are squared (and therefore parallel) to the line of putt.

Figure 13. Stance

2. HEAD AND EYES. The position of the head is very important—
it determines the position of your eyes. When putting, your eyes
should be directly over the ball and parallel to the line of putt. If your
eyes are not directly over the ball, move your head so that your eyes
are in the correct position. If you lean too far forward, your eyes will
be beyond the ball, and you'll push putts to the left. If you're standing
more erect and your eyes are inside the line of putt, you'll push putts
to the right. Keep your head still and let your eyes follow the ball
toward the hole after the stroke. I repeat, Don't move your head. If
you become overeager to see where your ball is going, it will affect
your follow-through, generally causing a poor shot.

STANCE IN WINDY CONDITIONS

Not many Weekend Golfers consider the effect of wind on their putt. Many tend to putt badly in the wind because they allow it to affect their stance and the result is nearly always an off-center hit and an unsuccessful putt. Wind can dry the putting green, thus making the ball roll farther than normal. Wind can push or hold back a ball that is rolling across a green. A strong wind can make it difficult to maintain a secure stance.

When setting up your putt in the wind, be patient, take careful aim, widen your stance to gain better balance, lower your grip a few inches on the putter handle, and concentrate harder than ever to keep your head still and your eyes over the ball. Crouch low to anchor yourself. Take a short, firm stroke. On the backstroke, increase your control by fixing your eyes on the ball and keeping the motion short. On the forward stroke, hit the ball especially hard while maintaining a firm grip. If the wind is gusty, crouch even lower, take an even wider stance, and use a very firm stroke.

3. GRIP. Grip is the way you maintain your hold on the putter handle. It helps push the putterhead slowly and consistently through the ball. In the ideal grip, the palms of the hands oppose each other and the thumbs are perpendicular to the putterhead. The palms act as a team; the right palm and the back of the left hand must face along the line of putt. You must maintain equal balance between the hands to execute a stroke that propels the ball forward along the correct line of putt.

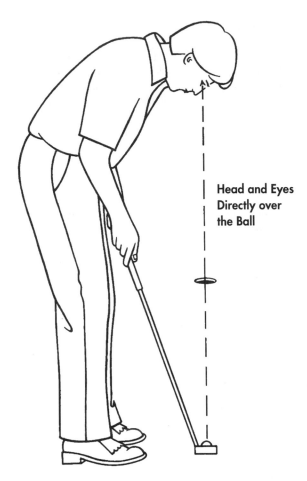

**Head and Eyes
Directly over
the Ball**

TEST YOUR POSITION—A SIMPLE TEST

Are you positioned correctly? One simple test is to drop a coin from the top of your nose—it should land on the ball. Another test is to dangle the putter directly under your nose—it should hang directly over the ball. If you fail either of these tests, position yourself so you can pass the test.

Figure 14. Eye and Head Position

A. Grip Pressure. How tightly you hold the putter in your hands can mean the difference in hitting the ball straight on or pushing it to the right or left. You must maintain nearly equal pressure between the hands, with the right hand gripping a little lighter than the left. The grip pressure must be constant throughout the stroke. If your right-hand grip is too tight, you'll pull the putterhead to the left. If your left-hand grip is too tight, you'll pull the putterhead to the right. Gripping the putter too tightly can also cause muscle tension and rigidity in the arms and the body.

B. Putting Grip. The most commonly used grip is the *reverse-overlap grip*. Other grips can be used but this is the preferred standard that gives you the most control of the putterhead. The method follows:

(1) Place the palm of your left hand on the left side of the putter, two inches from the top of the putter handle. The back of the left hand must be square with the blade of the putter and with the line of putt. The left hand guides the stroke. Look down—if you can see the first knuckle of your left hand, you know you have the proper hand position.

(2) Place the palm of the right-hand opposite the palm of the left hand (palms parallel to each other). The key is to have the right palm face along the line of putt. It becomes an easy matter to move your right palm toward the line of putt instead of concentrating on putterhead alignment. If the palms face to the left or right of the line of putt, you'll miss the putt and consequently, you'll miss the hole.

(3) The forefinger of the left hand should overlap the fourth finger of the right hand, hence, the name, reverse-overlap grip.

(4) The thumbs of both hands extend straight down the top of the putter shaft. Most putters have a flat surface on the grip handle to minimize the possibility of turning the putterhead at any time during the stroke.

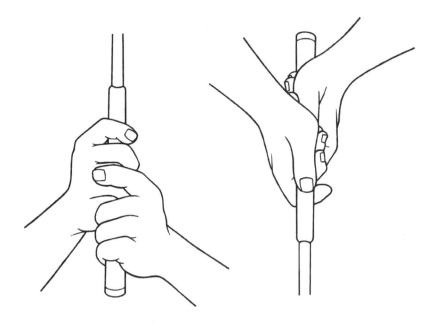

Figure 15. Reverse-overlap Grip

4. HANDS. The position of your hands plays an important role in aligning the putterhead with the ball and the line of putt. The hands should be kept slightly ahead of the ball. With this forward press, you'll produce a peppy beginning for your backstroke. It's the hands' job to keep the putterface in a square position throughout the back-stroke and forward stroke. If you let your hands get behind the ball, you may develop a wrist stroke—resulting in a weak grip position and unpredictable results.

CLUB POSITION

Now that you know how to take your stance, position your head and eyes, and grip the putter, you must align the putterhead and ball with the line of putt and your stance.

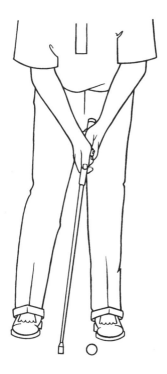

Figure 16. Forward Press of Hands

1. ALIGNMENT OF PUTTERHEAD WITH LINE OF PUTT. Putter-head alignment is a critical part of the putting setup. The putterhead must be at right angles to the line of putt to properly propel the ball along that line. If the putterhead is turned right or left, and does not face down the line of putt, it'll be difficult to make the shot. Alignment will be lost and the putterface will cut or slice the ball on impact causing a miss. With the hole being more than 2 times wider than the ball, you can miss your line of putt slightly on short putts and still put the ball into the hole. The hole will appear even wider when you consider that your ball can drop into the hole if just half of the ball crosses the edge of the hole. As you move farther away from the hole, a small error in alignment can turn into a major miss.

Parallel and at
right angles to
line of putt

Figure 17. Putterhead Aligned with Line of Putt

2. PUTTER SOLE POSITION. The putter sole (bottom of putter-head) must be completely flush with the surface of the green. This position won't be a problem if you purchased your putter with the flatness of the sole in mind; it should lie flat naturally when you set up to putt. It's easy to carelessly tilt the sole up or down—so be sure to check the flatness of the sole each time you set up. An improper sole position can cause you to scuff the ground with whichever end of the blade is lower. As Dave Pelz puts it in *Putt Like the Pros*, "If the putter sits on the heel and you happen to scuff the ground slightly before impact, the heel will slow down as it hits the turf and the toe will flip forward. And your putt will roll badly off line to the left. Conversely players who scuff the toe tend to miss putts in the opposite direction, to the right." Continuing, Pelz adds, "The best solution is

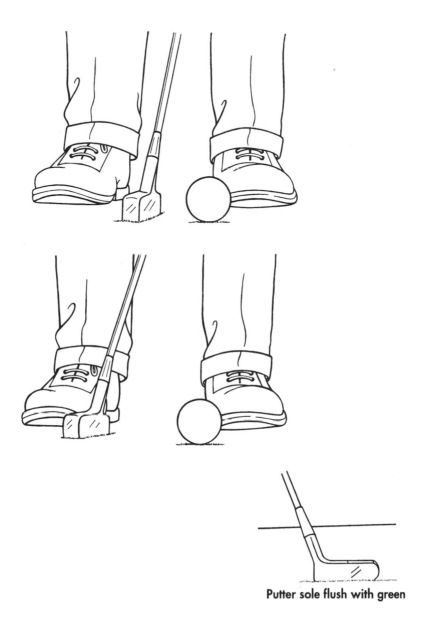

Putter sole flush with green

Figure 18. Putter Sole Position

to find a putter that sits flat on the ground when you assume your normal address position."

3. ALIGNMENT OF BALL WITH PUTTERHEAD. The ball is normally positioned opposite the *sweet spot*, or approximate center of the putterhead. The *sweet spot* is the point on the putterface where there is no vibration when the ball hits the point straight on. Golf pros argue that if you hit the ball from any other spot, vibrations will occur and cause the ball to veer off its intended line. I, personally, cannot tell the difference. Maybe vibrations occur and maybe they don't. But whatever the case, I don't think it'll make any difference to you, the average Weekend Golfer. Thus, I have developed an alternate ball position for the alignment of the ball with the putterhead.

 AN ALTERNATE BALL POSITION

I have found that you can achieve remarkable solidity when playing the ball from the back part of the putterface (near the heel), rather than from opposite the sweet spot. It's easy to position yourself to hit off the back part of the putter. Hitting off the sweet spot is not so easy because it's not in the same place on all putters and when taking your stroke, you can't always keep the ball on line with the sweet spot. A slight twist of the putterface will cause a mishit. It takes good memory and muscle coordination to consistently hit the sweet spot every time.

How to achieve this alternate ball position. Position the ball between the heel and the center of the putterhead—the center is usually marked with a single line or groove. The key is to keep the ball close to the heel of the putter. With the ball impacting so close to the shaft you get an added feeling of solidity. Position your ball in the center of your line of putt, or channel. Recalling from Chapter 2 how the line of putt is really a channel, this alternate ball position is simply a refine-

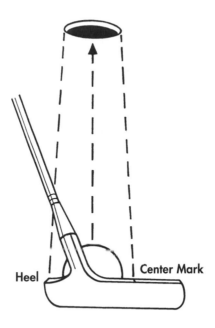

Heel   Center Mark

Figure 19. Alignment of Ball Between Heel & Center Mark

ment of the channel that will help you to aim more precisely. You can align the single line or groove on the putterhead with the right side of the channel. The end of the putterhead (heel side) is aligned with the left side of the channel. This alignment is really simple. Try it on a straight putt first. Then work on breaking putts.

Regardless whether your putt is straight or has a break, you'll still align your putterhead with the right and left side of the channel. Your ball will sit in the center of the channel. On straight putts of three feet or less, align the center mark of the putter with the right edge of the hole. You can now be assured that you're on line. All you have to do is stroke the ball smoothly and correctly, and it should go into the hole nearly every time, barring any imperfections on the line itself.

While this alternate ball position works exceptionally well with short putts, it can also apply to longer putts.

Experiment to make sure that this method of positioning the ball away from the traditional sweet spot is good for you. Even if you have no trouble finding and hitting the sweet spot, at least try this new ball position. It should give you a stronger feeling when stroking the ball. I have taught this technique to many of my golfing friends and they have all noticed a significant difference in the way the putter feels. This alignment method is especially useful if you don't practice often. It's nice to have a feeling of assurance when positioning the ball for putting especially when you play golf infrequently.

4. ALIGNMENT OF BALL MARKINGS WITH PUTTERHEAD AND LINE OF PUTT. Another ball alignment trick is to position the printed manufacturer's name at right angles to your putterhead. This is such a simple and effective alignment method that it's surprising how few authors mention it. Start by aligning the manufacturer's name printed on the ball (or in the case of specialty balls, whatever is printed across the center of the ball) so that the printed line is at right angles to your putterhead and points along the line of putt. If you have trouble aligning the printed name with the line of putt, step back a few feet and you'll get a better perspective. The name actually becomes the starting point for the line of putt. It becomes easy to start and stay on line when you have the ball, putterhead, and line of putt in perfect alignment. If you like this method, you might consider buying balls with a long name printed across their circumference for easy visual reference.

5. ALIGNMENT OF BALL WITH HEEL OF LEFT FOOT. For nearly all putts, place the ball in line with the heel of the left foot. This does not mean from the toe or somewhere off the left foot—it means to align the ball off the heel of the left foot. You must be fairly exact. Just envision a straight line from your heel to your ball. Keep this line at right angles to your line of putt.

Be careful—if your stance and putterhead are not square to your line of putt, it's difficult to align the ball properly. Depending on how you're lined up, your ball may actually be in the center of your stance, when you think it's off your left foot. If the ball is too close to the

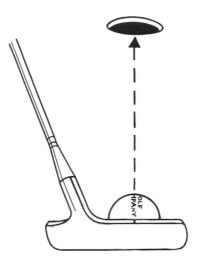

Figure 20. Alignment of Ball Name with Line of Putt

center of your stance, your stroke may cause backspin instead of the desired overspin. And if you go to the other extreme and place the ball too far forward in your stance, you'll have the tendency to pull the ball left or right. In either case, you must make sure that your feet are positioned parallel to the line of putt.

STANDARD PUTTER TYPES

Selecting a putter that matches your putting style is an important part in the way you set up to putt. When choosing a putter, you should be concerned with the shape of the putterhead, shaft length, handle thickness, and the angle between the shaft and putterhead (this ensures the putter sole is flat at setup). While there are many putter designs, there are three standard types. They are generally categorized by putterhead type—the most popular styles being the *straight blade, flange*

This is the golfer's eye view of a putt. Your eyes should be fixed on the back of the ball. Your head should remain motionless throughout the stroke and long after the ball has been sent rolling on its line.

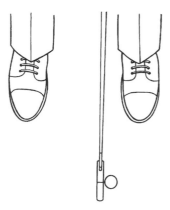

Figure 21. Alignment of Ball Off Left Heel

blade, and the *mallet head*. The majority of all other putters are based on one of these shapes.

1. STRAIGHT BLADE. A thin, lightweight putterhead. It's useful for putting on fast greens where it doesn't take much weight to get the ball rolling.

2. FLANGE BLADE. A basic straight blade with a massive amount of weight (flange) added to the back. The flange is often hollowed out in spots. The cavities allow the designer to put more weight at the bottom of the head and around the perimeter. This is currently a very popular putter among the golf pros and is the one I prefer to use for my putting style. It works especially well for plumb-bobbing, aligning the ball with the putterhead using the alternate alignment position, and for putting from off the green.

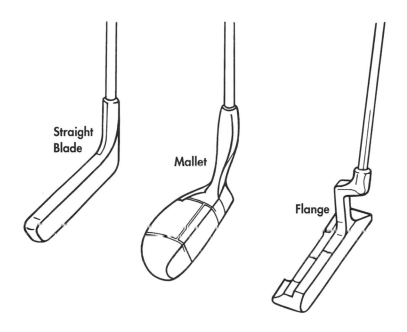

Figure 22. Standard Putter Types

3. MALLET HEAD.   A variation of the straight blade having a half-moon–shaped putterhead. This putter is the heaviest of the three standard types and is the preferred choice for use on slow greens or in windy conditions.

A putterhead can be made from wood, steel, or aluminum. The putter shaft is generally 33 to 36 inches in length and can be made of wood, steel, graphite, fiberglass, titanium, or plastic. Type of material is your choice. The handle typically has a flat or square surface so the thumbs can lie flat along its center. The putter handle should be as thick as possible for proper control. If the handle is too small your hands will become too active, which may cause a wristy stroke and uncertain results.

Putter choice is a matter of personal preference. You can choose any type, but your choice could make the difference between becoming a good or a superb putter. Most golf pros use standard putters—so you should too. Try each standard type but remember to buy one that lies flat naturally when you set up to putt.

DON'T BUY PUTTERS THROUGH MAIL ORDER

Regardless of which putter you select, it is important that you test it before buying. You need to be able to pick it up, grip it, and take some practice strokes to make sure it feels good to you and that the putting sole lies flat naturally. When buying a putter through the mail, you can't test it until it's delivered to you. So if you see a putter advertised, call the manufacturer and ask for the location of the nearest distributor in your area. Do yourself a favor—don't buy the putter blindly.

Unfortunately, some day in your life, you are likely to fall for one of those catchy magazine ads boasting that a certain putter (usually weighted or oddly shaped) is the answer to your putting problems. Each manufacturer will proclaim that its putter has been scientifically proven to make the perfect putt. But remember—it's not the putter that makes the shot, it's you and your hand and eye coordination. Stay alert. How many golf pros routinely use unusual putters? Most golfers use either a standard straight blade or a flange blade putter. The serious golfer will typically use a standard putter rather than select one that is supposed to perform miracles all by itself.

If you still want to buy a putter that looks pretty or feels lucky, then do yourself a favor and buy one that feels balanced so you can stroke it smoothly, use it in plumb-bobbing, and from off the green. Remember that if you have a lucky putter and you're lucky all the time, it's your confidence and putting style that are making the putt.

CHAPTER 4

Stroking the Ball

YOU'RE NOW READY TO HIT THE BALL

The final line of putt has been determined, you've set up the putt, and now you're ready to roll the ball into the hole. To do this, you must first learn to estimate distance and then to stroke the ball. Learning to estimate distance takes a lot of practice and confidence; learning to stroke the ball is relatively simple. We'll first address how to stroke the ball and then how to estimate distance.

PUTTING STROKE DEFINED

According to the *USGA's Golf Rules in Pictures*, a stroke may be defined as "The forward movement of the club made with the intention of fairly striking at and moving the ball." A putting stroke is the means by which a golfer uses a putter to propel the ball toward a hole.

The essence of a good stroke is to have the putterhead, moving along the initial line of putt, gradually gaining speed as it comes in contact with the ball. The face of the putterhead must be square with the intended line of putt when the ball is struck. The lengths of the backstroke and forward stroke are nearly identical. This kind of balance promotes a smooth and even stroke. Perhaps the worst mistake that can be made is to rotate the putterface during the backstroke. Your alignment and the putterface will cut or slice the ball at the point of impact, preventing the desirable overspin.

The ball can be stroked in several ways: jabbed, punched, pushed, or swept. A sweeping motion is the preferred stroke for moving the ball in a smooth, rhythmic, and fluid motion. There are two popular stroking methods: the arms-and-shoulders stroke and the wrist stroke. The arms-and-shoulders stroke is the one I recommend in this book.

1. ARMS-AND-SHOULDERS STROKE. This stroke is much like a pendulum sweeping motion: the hands, arms, and shoulders move together. The entire action should be automatic. You're moving the putterhead within the confines of the pendulum swing; you're not manipulating the putterhead in any other way. The left arm guides the putterhead backward the appropriate distance, and the right arm takes the putterhead through the moment of contact with the ball and then continues toward the target after impact.

The key to this technique is to keep the wrist break to a minimum. Throughout the stroke the wrists remain locked. The backstroke should move in a straight line to ensure the ball is struck on its center, resulting in an overspinning ball that hugs the green. Note that the head stays down well after impact. Lifting the head early will cause the shoulders to turn, thus spoiling the putt. Overspin reduces the chance of the ball spinning off line. With the arms-and-shoulders technique it's possible to develop precise swing measurements, enabling you to accurately estimate distance.

2. WRIST STROKE. The wrist stroke is more like a punch or a jab than the sweeping action of the arms-and-shoulders technique. This stroke uses wrist action to propel the ball forward. It enhances your sense of touch because the hands are more sensitive than the arms and shoulders. The right hand does most of the work; both wrists hinge slightly on the backstroke. The right hand helps accelerate the putterhead into the ball.

The major pitfall of the wrist stroke is that it's difficult to determine how much wrist action, or feel, is needed to propel a ball forward.

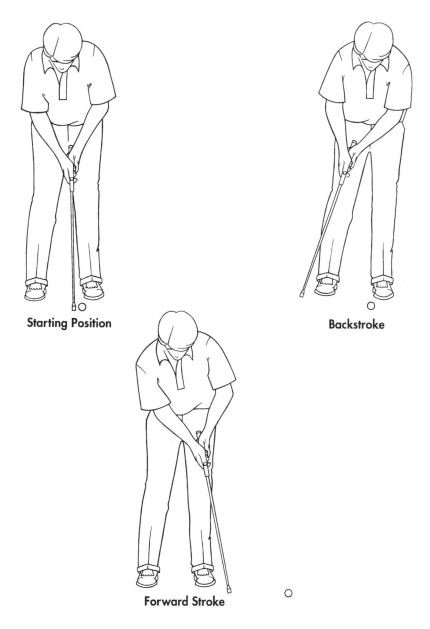

Starting Position

Backstroke

Forward Stroke

Figure 23. Arms-and-Shoulders Putting Stroke

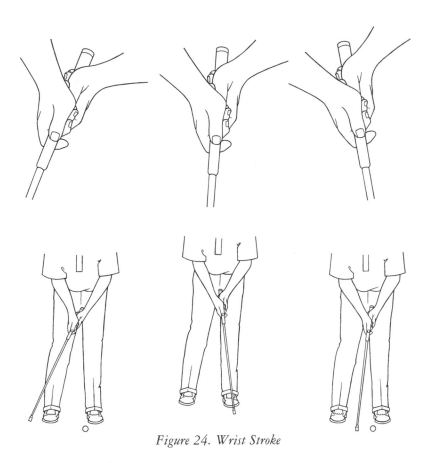

Figure 24. Wrist Stroke

It's the hinging of the wrists that controls the strength required to propel the ball toward the hole. Because of the feel required, the wrist stroke is not recommended. It's difficult to be scientific if you're worrying about *feel*.

ACCELERATING THE PUTTERHEAD AT IMPACT

While moving your putterhead in a smooth, fluid manner, you must learn to accelerate the speed of the putterhead at impact with the ball.

This causes the ball to move forward at a steady pace—a critical goal of your putting stroke. The key to smooth putting is even tempo. You must take a short backstroke and make a positive movement forward. Taking a long backstroke and slowing down the putterhead as it approaches the ball often results in an uneven tempo.

SLOWING DOWN THE PUTTER-
HEAD AT IMPACT IS ONE OF
THE MOST COMMON
MISTAKES COMMITTED BY A
WEEKEND GOLFER.

In the forward movement, the putterhead should be kept low and the left wrist rigid, allowing no break. At the same time, the back of the left hand as well as the palm of the right hand should stay at right angles to the line of putt. The left hand and wrist are carried through the stroke in a square position. This is the accelerating stroke. Lee Trevino gives a helpful hint in *Groove Your Swing My Way* for keeping the wrists rigid on the forward stroke: "Accelerate the left arm through the ball on all putts, so the left wrist does not cup inward." Be careful to accelerate the left hand and arm forward on all strokes, so that the right hand doesn't take over and flip the putterhead upward or off line.

You can relate this concept of accelerating to depressing the gas pedal in a car. The harder you press the pedal, the quicker the car moves. If you press the pedal at one time and ease off at another, your ride will be jerky, and your passengers will wonder where you got your driver's license. When driving, you must maintain a steady pressure on the pedal to keep the car moving smoothly—and to keep the police from thinking you've had a little too much to drink. With golf, you must keep a constant pressure on the putterhead to keep it moving forward on a steady course. If you accelerate through the ball one time and not the next, you won't be able to consistently control how far the ball will roll.

Most putting problems are caused when the stroke speed is uneven or when the putterhead decreases speed on impact with the ball. Ac-

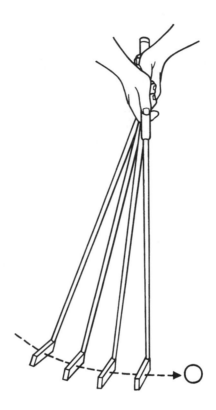

Figure 25. Acceleration

celerating one time and decelerating the next will result in inconsistent putting, and unless you recognize the cause and correct the problem, your overall game will suffer. It's easy to get trapped into decelerating into the ball because there is fear of hitting the ball too hard. A ball that is slowing down will react to the slightest slope and imperfection on the putting surface, and distance and direction become uncertain. To roll the ball smooth and straight, the putterhead must accelerate at an even pace through the ball.

ESTIMATING THE DISTANCE FROM BALL TO HOLE

According to *Webster's Tenth New Collegiate Dictionary*, distance is defined as "the degree or amount of separation between two points, lines, or objects measured along the shortest path joining them." In this case, the two objects are the ball and the hole. Estimating distance, or the amount of separation between the ball and hole, is not as easy as it seems. Deciding how hard to hit the ball along your line of putt to reach the hole is a challenge. Golf pros have admitted that it's difficult to tell someone how to hit a ball 30 or 50 feet. Golf pros spend so many hours with the putter day in and day out that they rely mostly on experience to make the ball roll the desired distance. You can't teach experience. Your aim, setup, and alignment could all be perfect but if you can't roll the ball the proper distance, you don't have a prayer of sinking a putt.

When you are ready to take your actual stroke, there are five points to consider: selecting a spot to shoot at, rolling the ball the right distance, lagging putts into an imaginary target, aiming for the "Pro" side of the hole, and sinking the putt. Each point is discussed in the next few pages.

1. SELECTING A SPOT TO SHOOT AT. On all putts, you should aim at a spot and not the hole. This is a key point that you must not forget. A spot is picked only after the line of putt is determined. Spot putting is important because you can shoot at a target not far from the position of your ball and know that if the ball crosses over the spot (or aim point), the ball will be on line and headed toward the hole.

Without a spot, it becomes difficult to consistently keep a ball headed along its intended line. As in bowling, it's easier to aim at and hit a target (spot) close to you rather than a target (pins) that is some distance away. Hence, the name "spot" bowling. In putting, your spot could be a small discoloration on the green, an old divot mark, or something distinguishing next to or along the proposed line of putt. Keep the spot near the ball—from 3 to 12 inches away. Otherwise, it'll be difficult to keep your eyes on the ball and watch the spot at the same time

Parallel and at
right angles to
line of putt

Player selects spot along line of putt and aligns himself to the spot, not the hole.

Figure 26. Spot Putting

without moving your head. Move your spot closer to the ball if the length of the putt warrants it—as in the case of an 8-inch putt.

2. ROLLING THE BALL THE CORRECT DISTANCE. If you can't hit the ball hard enough, it'll never have a chance of going in the hole. This is the premise for the adage, "Never Up, Never In." John Garrity, author of *Putting, The Stroke-Saver's Guide,* has developed an effective technique for propelling the ball precise distances. He says, "Fortunately, there are ways to improve your distance control, even if you've the proverbial 'touch of a blacksmith.' " Garrity has developed a formula whereby you can take a precise backstroke to propel a ball a certain distance. Garrity continues, "One foot equals one inch. You take the putter back 4 inches for a 4-foot putt, 10 inches for a 10-

foot putt, 20 inches for a 20-foot putt, and so on. You can practice with a yardstick laid on the ground or on a carpet. Don't worry about how far the ball actually rolls. Just practice making strokes of different lengths, taking care that the stroke is rhythmic, fluid, and unhurried and that each forward stroke is the same length as the backstroke." Practice these different putts and see for yourself if the measurements recommended by Garrity are accurate. I think you'll be pleasantly surprised. Watch the golf pros. See what they do.

With long putts, Garrity says, "One foot equals one inch works well until you're 30 feet or more from the hole. At that range, it's hard to tell how far back you're taking the putter because the putter-head is high off the ground and inside the line. What's more, really long putts call for some wrist action to get the ball into the hole."

To conclude, Garrity says, "Great players don't use cut-and-dried formulas. They rely on feel. But watch them! Their strokes normally conform to the one foot equals one inch formula—adjusted of course, for the faster greens they putt on."

3. LAGGING PUTTS INTO AN IMAGINARY TARGET. Learning to estimate how far a ball will roll is especially important on putts over 15 feet. Many of the golf pros advocate shooting at an imaginary target, with the hole being the bull's-eye. Instead of just hitting the ball in the direction of the hole, you want your ball to move slowly, or lag, into an imaginary circle and stop. On putts between 15 and 30 feet, this imaginary target could have a 3-foot diameter. Then your next putt would be no more than one-half the diameter of the circle, or within a maximum of 1½ feet of the hole. An easy way to visualize this target area is to place tees about 1½ feet to the left and right of the hole with the hole being in the middle. Your objective is to lag balls into the target area. If you sink the ball, all the better. On putts over 30 feet, you may wish to enlarge this target to a 6-foot diameter; thus, your next putt would be 3 feet or less. It's really easy. After some practice, it shouldn't be too difficult to roll that tiny ball into a 3-or 6-foot diameter target area from almost any distance. Of course, the theory is that you can make any shot from within the target area. As you become a better putter, you may want to reduce the diameter of your imaginary target, thus making your next putt even shorter.

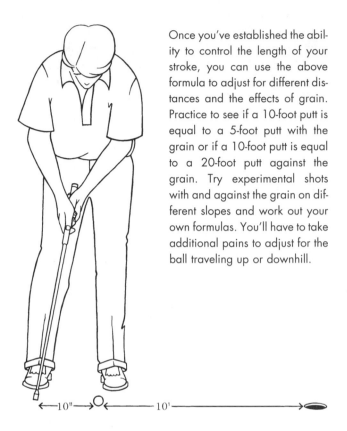

Once you've established the ability to control the length of your stroke, you can use the above formula to adjust for different distances and the effects of grain. Practice to see if a 10-foot putt is equal to a 5-foot putt with the grain or if a 10-foot putt is equal to a 20-foot putt against the grain. Try experimental shots with and against the grain on different slopes and work out your own formulas. You'll have to take additional pains to adjust for the ball traveling up or downhill.

←—10"—→O←——— 10' ———————→

Player takes Backstroke of 10 inches to putt 10 feet (considering no grain).

Figure 27. Rolling the Ball the Correct Distance

After consistently landing in your target, you can worry about where the ball lands inside the target area.

4. AIMING FOR THE *PRO* NOT THE *AMATEUR* SIDE OF THE HOLE. Golf pros aim for the high side of the break. The high side is called the *pro* side of the hole because golf pros always take full account of slope and if they miss the hole on a putt with a break, the

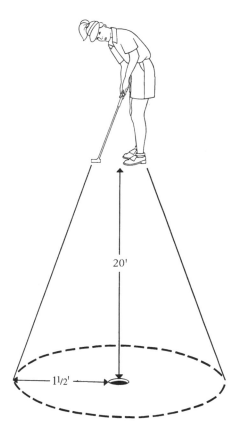

20'

1½'

Figure 28. Imaginary Target

ball will miss on the side above the hole. As you'll find out, playing the high side will increase your probability of making your putts.

If a putt has a right-to-left break, the *pro* side is to the right side of the hole. If a putt has a left-to-right break, the *pro* side is to the left side of the hole. Experiment with this concept. You'll quickly realize that playing the *pro* side increases your chances of making putts.

If you err on the low side of the break, you won't make the putt. The low side of the hole is called the *amateur* side because amateurs tend to underestimate the effect of slope on the green and often let the ball dribble below the hole. If a putt rolls to the low side of the hole, you have *no chance* of making the putt under any circumstances. This is where acceleration through impact pays off. If you hit the ball firmly, you're more likely to err on the *pro* side than to dribble down to the *amateur* side of the hole.

5. SINKING THE PUTT. Keep your head still, hit the ball, and don't move your head until you have completed your forward stroke. Wait until you hear your ball drop into the hole—then move. If you don't hear it drop within 5 to 10 seconds, look up to see how far it rolled. Whatever you do, you must resist the temptation to look up before the completion of your stroke, no matter how short the putt.

BASIC PUTTING LIES

There are six basic putting lies. These include the short, long, uphill, downhill, sidehill, and the straight putt—and there are many variations. Different authors suggest different distances for short, medium, and long putts. You must decide on your own distances. To most, including myself, a short putt is 3 feet or less; to others, a short putt could be 6 to 10 feet. A long putt is typically 30 feet or more but to someone who can't putt well, a long putt could be anything over 6 feet in length. You have to be your own judge.

Whatever the distances, the setups and stroke advice offered in the next few pages apply to the six basic putting lies. When reading this section, it's assumed that you have found your line of putt, selected a spot to aim at along that line of putt, and are ready to set up and stroke the ball the correct distance.

1. SHORT PUTT. A short putt is one in which the ball usually lies within 3 feet of the hole.

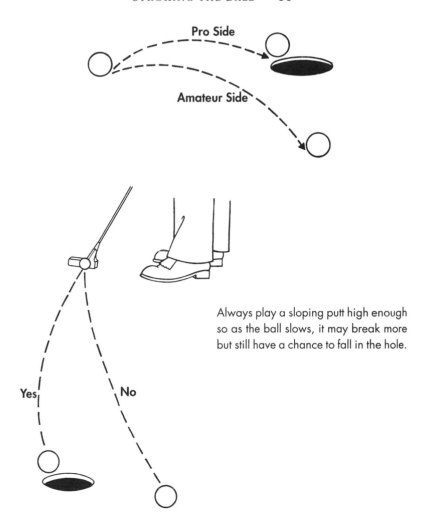

Always play a sloping putt high enough so as the ball slows, it may break more but still have a chance to fall in the hole.

Figure 29. Pro *vs.* Amateur *Side of the Hole*

THE GOAL OF A SHORT PUTT IS
TO PUT THE BALL INTO THE HOLE
IN ONE STROKE.

When you are ready to stroke the ball, find a spot a few inches in front of your ball on the line of putt. Visualize your ball rolling over the spot, continuing along the line of putt, and into the hole.

On these short putts, use the standard setup. Execute a firm forward stroke and listen to the ball drop before moving your body or raising your head. Watch your stroke speed. Many golfers have the tendency to decelerate on short putts, rather than hit the ball firm like any other putt. A decelerating ball can easily be affected by the slope of the green or any imperfection that may be on the line of putt.

If you're missing most of your short putts, try making an exaggerated forward stroke by moving the putterhead a few inches farther than normal, along the line of putt. You can also try playing the ball farther back in your stance. This makes the distance between the ball and hole seem shorter because your body is actually closer to the hole. Be bold and hit the short putt firmly.

While the short putt should be relatively easy, it's the putt on which most golfers experience a serious case of the jitters. A slight movement of the head, a misguided putterhead, a misreading of the green or grain, poor judgment of distance, or tension can make you miss. A discussion of the jitters, often referred to as the *"yips,"* follows at the end of this chapter.

2. LONG PUTT.   A long putt is any putt in which a ball lies more than 30 feet from the hole. The goal of a long putt is to get close to the hole. To sink a long putt is an accomplishment. Trying to sink long putts in one shot is not realistic and this can result in one too many 3-putt greens.

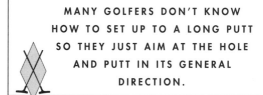

MANY GOLFERS DON'T KNOW
HOW TO SET UP TO A LONG PUTT
SO THEY JUST AIM AT THE HOLE
AND PUTT IN ITS GENERAL
DIRECTION.

For long putts, your stance should be slightly different from the standard. Stand taller and straighter. It's easier to judge the correct distance on a long putt from a more erect position. If you make a mistake and crouch too low, you'll need to bend your wrists to accommodate the long backstroke and forward stroke needed to propel the ball into the hole—possibly resulting in a jerky stroke and a missed putt. Select a spot along the line of putt, about 8 inches from your ball. Aim for the *pro* side of the hole and accelerate through impact.

STAND MORE ERECT
ON LONG PUTTS.

Without a compelling reason to make a long putt, such as to win a hole or game, play realistically and aim for the imaginary 3-or 6-foot diameter target area. Your goal is to get close and if you're anywhere within the target area, your next putt should be relatively easy. If you've spent time practicing the short putt, there is a good chance you can sink your ball anywhere from within the imaginary target area.

3. UPHILL PUTT. An uphill putt is any putt in which the hole is above the ball. The steeper the hill, the harder you have to hit the ball. With the hole being on a slope facing you, the back of the hole is higher than the front edge and actually makes the hole an easier target than usual. This is why golf pros prefer the uphill putt over other putts—there is more hole to shoot at and the chances of sinking the ball into the hole are higher. And to make this shot even easier, balls will break less on uphill shots. For these reasons, the uphill putt is actually one of the easiest in golf. You can be bold and hit an aggressive shot toward the hole, knowing that your ball has an excellent chance of going in or getting very close. The emphasis on an uphill putt is firmness, even boldness.

The average golfer generally doesn't hit the ball hard enough when putting uphill. Try this. Visualize a hole just behind the real one and aim for the new imaginary hole. This will give you a stronger stroke on uphill putts. If you are *still* not hitting hard enough, move your imaginary hole farther above the real one. With this technique, you should now reach the vicinity of the hole nearly every time and have an excellent chance of sinking the putt.

For uphill putts, position the ball farther back in your stance, close to the center. If the ball is in its standard position, off the left heel, the rising putterface will hit the ball, causing the ball to bounce, or quickly slow down before it reaches the hole. The key to uphill putts is to grip the putter more firmly than normal and to accelerate a little more than usual at impact. Practice this.

4. DOWNHILL PUTT. A downhill putt is any putt in which your ball lies above the hole. It's one of the toughest putts in the game of golf because it's so difficult to control the downhill speed of the ball. It takes only a small error in judgment to finish very short or very long, which could set you up to take another two or three putts. With the fear of stroking the ball too firmly, you tend to decelerate at impact, forcing the ball off its intended line, causing it to fall short, or to miss the hole. On the other hand, if you take too long a backstroke and accelerate too much on impact, you're likely to propel the ball well past the hole. One technique is to take a shorter backstroke so you can still accelerate through the ball. Another technique is to visualize how far your ball will roll naturally and then hit it a little harder. You'll soon get the hang of it.

You cannot expect to make many downhill putts. Just try to get close enough so you can make your next putt drop in. Your strategy could be to putt the ball beyond the hole so that your second shot is uphill, a much easier shot to make. Experiment with the effect of break on downhill shots because the ball will break a little more on them. Practice this. It's a delicate maneuver. The emphasis on downhill putts should be a lightness of touch and steady nerves.

Luck will make a few of the downhill putts—but your real goal is to avoid hitting the ball too far past the hole. If you're still uncertain about ball speed on downhill putts, try Lee Trevino's advice from his videotape *Putt for Dough*: "Just take aim and putt and don't even think about taking a practice swing." Try it. I did and his advice has possibilities. If you don't think too long about a shot and nervousness doesn't have time to set in, you can judge ball speed with amazing accuracy.

5. SIDEHILL PUTT.   A sidehill putt is any putt in which a ball will travel onto a slope and break right-to-left or left-to-right to reach the hole. In actuality, a sidehill putt is a combination of an uphill and a downhill putt. Select a spot about 6 inches from your ball and be very careful to enter the line of putt precisely. On a right-to-left putt, you have to hit the ball onto the slope to your right and let the ball break (turn down) toward the hole. On a left-to-right putt, you have to hit the ball onto the slope to your left and let the ball break toward the hole. On both of these putts, you must shoot up to the break point, at which time the ball will turn downhill toward the hole. If you hit the ball too gently, you won't reach the break point. If you hit it too hard, you'll go beyond the break point. In both cases, you'll miss the hole. This is why aim and speed are so important on sidehill putts.

Setup to the sidehill putt has to be very precise. If the ball is higher than your feet, your stance must be more erect than normal. Close your stance slightly and back up a little so you don't crowd the ball. For this right-to-left breaking putt, play the ball back toward the center of your stance. Keep your eyes over the ball and make sure the putterhead is square to the line of putt and that the putter sole is flat.

If the ball is lower than your feet, stand closer to the ball and crouch over more. A small error can result in a major miss. For this left-to-right breaking putt, play the ball off your left toe. Open your stance slightly and put a little more weight on your left foot. Move your hands forward toward the line of putt while keeping the putterhead stationary, with its sole flat on the green's surface, and at right angles to the line of putt. With a firm stroke, you'll be able to send the ball over your selected spot at the right speed so your ball breaks into the hole.

Sidehill putts need a lot of practice. Making one can give you confidence in your putting and will impress partners and opponents alike. Sinking a sharp-breaking sidehill putt can be very rewarding, and it's fun as well.

6. STRAIGHT PUTT.   A straight putt is any putt in which there is no perceived break. While a straight putt can be any length, it's not likely to be longer than 6 feet because of slope, grain conditions, and green imperfections. This is the most difficult putt in the game of golf because there is no margin for error. This means you can't play the *pro* side of the hole because there is no break. And if you don't take correct aim, you'll miss the hole. Treat this putt like any other putt and set up to it using the standards recommended in this book. Pick a spot 3 or 4 inches in front of the ball. Keep your putterhead at right angles to your selected spot and the line of putt. Take the putterhead straight back and accelerate it toward your spot along the line of putt. Spot putting is especially important on the straight putt. Use it.

YIPS — ANXIETY WHEN PUTTING

A *"yip"* is a nervous condition suffered by golfers and characterized by twitching, hesitations, and jerky movements during putting. While yips are typically associated with short putts, golfers can be afflicted on any putt. Yips can be traced to being overly concerned with slope, ball speed, and grain. A case of the yips can cause anything to go wrong during the putting stroke. It can cause your eyes, head, and shoulders to move during your swing. It can even cause your mind to wander.

Golfers tend to put a great deal of pressure on themselves on short putts. Touring professional Dave Hill was once heard to comment that from "5 feet in to the hole, you're in the throw-up zone." Lee Trevino says his putter gets "as heavy as a wagon tongue" when he faces a big money putt. Undue pressure can cause golfers to freeze. When they do take a backstroke, they will often jab at the ball or decelerate on impact. The result is usually to miss the line of putt and invariably to miss the hole.

TIPS FOR OVERCOMING THE YIPS

1. Aim at a spot 3 to 6 inches from your ball along your line of putt. Place close attention to the spot and nothing else.

2. Increase your concentration, take a deep breath, and putt smoothly and slowly.

3. "Grip the putter as you normally would and wring it like a towel. The effort of twisting your hands toward each other helps to lessen tension." This suggestion actually makes the club feel lighter in your hands. The quote is from Lee Trevino's videotape *Putt for Dough*.

4. "Hold the putter lightly." This suggestion stems from the fact that the yips cause you to bear down on the putter handle as if to strangle it. The quote is from Vivien Saunders' *The Complete Book of Golf Practice*.

Of course, the best tension reliever is to know in your heart that you can make your short putts. This confidence will help to override those fears of missing a short putt. You'll be able to aim, setup, and promptly stroke the ball before the yips have a chance to set in.

CHAPTER 5

Putting from Off the Green

THE CONCEPT

The idea of putting from off the green isn't new. The pros do it. You've probably done it. But it's unlikely that you've ever considered it as part of your standard repertoire—those shots you call upon when selecting the correct club to use. When I putt from off the green, I hear statements like, "You've got to be kidding" or "I can't believe you're using your putter from that distance." My partners and opponents can't believe I'm able to reach the green most of the time just using my putter. And they are often amazed at my accuracy and at how close I get to the flag stick. They watch me, they see the results, *but* they shrug off my successes and continue using that traditional short iron. Even when their shots go sour, they still use the same club in the same situation time after time.

MANY GOLFERS ARE RELUCTANT
TO PUTT FROM OFF THE GREEN
BECAUSE TRADITION GUIDES
THEIR GAME.

They think there are too many variables that may cause a ball to fall short of its target when putted from off the green. The putterhead could get caught in the grass on the backstroke, the ball might meet resistance when rolling through heavy grass, or it could roll over a bump, tree root, or fall into a hole. But I, and others, including golf pros, have found considerable success in using the putter from off the green. Once you develop your new putting style, you'll discover that putting from off the green is reliable and quite accurate—more so than using the traditional short irons. You'll see. I personally find the putter to be the most effective shot in my short game.

Many of my golfing companions argue that the proper approach shot is to chip the ball with a short iron, or to run it onto the green with a long or middle iron. Chip shots are okay if you can consistently place your ball on the green and near the hole. But to be able to hit a chip shot straight every time and directly at the flag stick is great golf. If this type of play suits you, then you're *not* an average golfer. The average Weekend Golfer is not consistent or accurate when chipping. He commits too many mistakes, causing unnecessary shots to be taken. It's too easy to mishit the ball and send it anywhere but where it should go. I think there are *more* variables that can cause a chip shot to go wrong than those associated with putting from off the green.

Chipping is complicated. You must consider lie, wind, slope, body movement, hand position, eye coordination, backstroke, and follow-through. That's too much to remember. Too much can go wrong with a chip shot. It's basically the same shot used for woods and irons except that it takes a much shorter backswing. You probably don't play enough or have enough experience to execute this shot consistently.

You *will* hit an occasional good chip shot that goes where you intend. But frequently, you will either *chili-dip* or *skull* the ball, resulting in a wasted shot. These are two words that the average Weekend Golfer would like to forget. When you *chili-dip* a ball, you dig the clubface of your short iron into the ground before hitting the ball causing the ball to go a very short distance—often the divot goes farther! When you *skull* a shot, you strike the ball in such a way as to send it on a low trajectory over the green, or at least a long way from the hole. These are wasted shots. And it's so frustrating to waste shots!

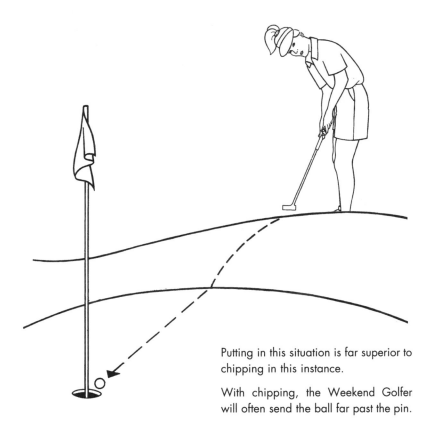

Putting in this situation is far superior to chipping in this instance.

With chipping, the Weekend Golfer will often send the ball far past the pin.

Figure 30. Putting vs. Chipping from Off the Green

It has probably never occurred to you to use the putter from off the green for a normal approach shot. Why continue to be wishful and chip from off the green when the putter is just waiting to be used. It's a simple, easy shot to execute and it greatly improves your chances of making it to the green. With the putter you have an excellent chance of directing the ball at the flag stick. You can't say the same for the chip shot. Your main goal is to get your ball onto the green, and with the putter it can be done. Once your approach shot with a putter becomes consistent, you can be more particular about ball placement. But for now, your primary objective is to get that little ball onto the putting surface, anywhere! Given these facts, it's only common sense to select the putter when making an approach shot.

I am not saying that you *have* to use your putter from off the green if you already execute a good chip shot. But if you have any reason to doubt your ability, I do suggest that you seriously consider the use of the putter *instead* of the traditional short iron for approach shots close to the green. Practice this shot.

THE METHOD FOR PUTTING FROM OFF THE GREEN

Treat this shot just as you would a standard putt with the exception of how hard you stroke the putter. You have to hit the ball firmer than normal to propel the ball through (or over) the grass and onto the green.

> USE THE SAME FAMILIAR TECHNIQUES FOR TAKING AIM, SETTING UP, AND STROKING THE BALL.

Don't forget to plumb-bob—it works as well from off the green as it does on the putting surface. Survey the lie and study the terrain you're putting across. Take your normal putting stance and position the ball opposite the heel of the left foot. Take a longer backstroke, accelerate at impact, and exaggerate the forward stroke. Without this increased effort to accelerate the putterhead, the ball will stop very quickly in the grass. With experience and patience, you'll soon learn how to putt from off the green from different lies and distances.

Take care to hit the ball solidly and smoothly. Don't jab or lunge in the effort to make the ball go farther. Once you're sure you can reach the green most of the time, you can use your knowledge of green conditions to get even closer to the flag stick. For instance, you can calculate how slope and grain may affect your ball as it rolls onto the green. You'll find that your goal will change from just stopping any-where on the green to stopping close to the flag stick. With practice, experience, and good results, you'll quickly realize the advantages of using the putter. You'll putt better from off the green and be happy to have found a successful alternative to using short irons for your approach shots.

There will be times when the flag stick will not be your target. For example, there may be a sand bunker or a tree between your ball and the flag stick. In such cases, you'll want to pick a line around these obstacles but still head for the green. As you start thinking creatively about your shots, you'll begin to appreciate the putter more.

WHEN TO PUTT FROM OFF THE GREEN

With your new shot-making abilities, there will be many situations when you *can* use your putter from off the green. No one lie will ever be the same. Some of the most common lies from which you'll want to use your putter are:

1. On the fringe of the green when the ball is sitting high on the grass. You just have to strike the ball a little harder to cause it to roll onto the green.

2. When the ball is on a mound or hill above the green. This is an easy putt because one small tap or push will send the ball downhill and toward the green. With a little practice, you'll find the putter is the only club you'll want to use from this position.

3. On a slope below the green. Just as for an uphill putt, you can be bold and hit the ball quite hard and it will travel directly toward the green.

4. When the ball is on open ground, on a dirt path, or when there is hard ground between you and the green. This shot can be executed from as far as 50 yards off the green. It's especially rewarding when the green is surrounded by many sand bunkers because you can nearly

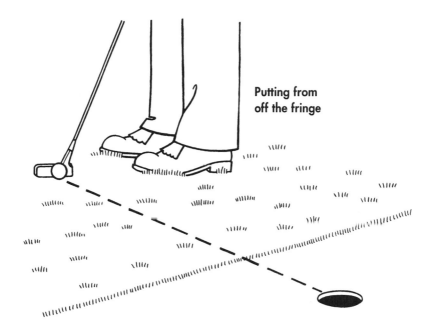

Putting from off the fringe

Figure 31. When to Putt from Off the Green

always putt your ball straight at the center of the green, thereby avoiding the sand bunkers.

In each of the above cases, a chip shot would normally be the choice for an average Weekend Golfer. But the putter is the better choice, as experience will show. There is just too much to remember when chipping. You have few fundamentals to remember with a putter and you can even carom a shot or play for bounces. Try that with a short iron.

WHEN *NOT* TO PUTT FROM OFF THE GREEN

There are some lies when the putter is not a good choice. It can still be used but it takes a lot of experience to use it in the following lies:

1. If the ball is sitting in high grass or the grass is wet, even a very hard stroke could leave your ball short of the green. It's difficult, but not impossible, to judge the impact of high or wet grass on a ball rolling toward the green.

2. When the ball is in a hole or something (tree root, rock, pole, etc.) prevents a smooth backstroke with the putter. In this case, some other club may be more effective.

3. When there is an obstacle (tree, bush, pole, or shed) or hazard between your ball and the green. A chip shot is the accepted shot in this case because you can fly your ball over the obstacle and onto the green. But you're not locked into a chip shot—you can still use your putter to go past or through the problem area. For instance, you can putt under a bush or you can play a tight line next to a light pole. Of course, you can't putt over water unless it is a narrow strip of water fairly level with the fairway and you hit the ball hard enough to skip over the water! But be careful, you'll probably skip over the green, too!

4. If you're so far from the green that even a hard stroke would leave you short. I have found that putting from over 15 yards off the green is chancy. It is possible to reach a green from as far as 80 yards with a putter, but the ground conditions between the ball and green must be ideal.

PUTTING FROM A SAND BUNKER

Putting from a sand bunker can be a good alternative to using a sand wedge if conditions are ideal. The average golfer rarely considers this

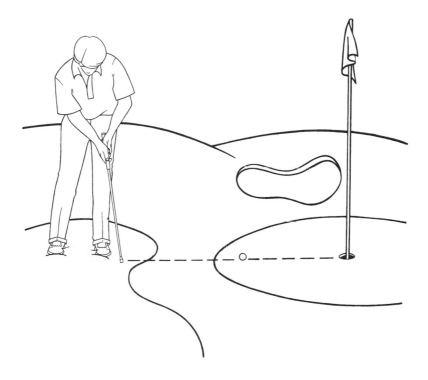

Figure 32. Putting from a Sand Bunker

shot because he doesn't know it's possible to putt out of sand. If you do choose to putt from a sand bunker, make sure the trap is flat, the sand firm, and that there is no overhanging lip between your ball and the green. And the ball must be sitting on top of the sand, not in it.

The method. Play the shot off the toe of the putterhead to reduce top spin, thus slowing the ball when it rolls onto the green. Move your grip farther down on the putter handle to guard against resting the putterhead on the sand and incurring a penalty stroke. Dig your feet into the sand, take a deep breath, and pray. In the rare case of a downhill lie, you may want to putt the ball away from the green to a safe lie and then putt back toward the green.

WHAT SOME PROFESSIONALS SAY ABOUT PUTTING FROM OFF THE GREEN

Seve Ballesteros, *Natural Golf*:

"Use your putter whenever possible. It takes an above-average chip to match an even average putt."

Ray Floyd, *From 60 Yards In*:

"I think the reason most people use a putter from off the green instead of a club with loft is that they don't have confidence in their chipping."

Jack Nicklaus, *Jack Nicklaus' Lesson Tee*:

"I will nearly always putt rather than chip from just off the green if the ground is firm and free from wet or heavy grass." Continuing he says, "I use my normal putting stroke, hitting it just a little more firmly than I would to cover the distance if it were entirely on the putting surface. One point I have to watch on these shots is head movement. It's a temptation any time you stroke harder than normal to look where it's going too soon!"

Gary Player, *Positive Golf*:

"When you have a close lie on bare ground or a good lie in smooth fringe, the putter can be the safest and most effective club to use, even though you have to roll the ball up and over the bank of the green. Don't be ashamed to putt, if that is your safest shot."

Chi Chi Rodriguez, *101 Super Shots*:

". . . You're making a very serious mistake if you reach for 'your' club every time you confront a chip, no matter how difficult or unique the lie of the ball. For example, if your ball sits 40 feet in front of the green on bare ground, and a threadbare hillock is in between you and the green, then you're much better off tackling this situation with the 'Texas Wedge,' the putter—and playing this *roller-coaster* shot. No doubt, this advice surprises you golfers who only believe a putter is to be used on the green. Well, it can also be your weapon for shots from off the green, too, as in the course situation already cited. Instead of taking a seven-iron or another lofted club and worrying about making precise, clean contact from a very thin lie, simply take your putter and make a dead-wristed backswing. On the downswing, incorporate a little exaggerated, lively wrist action into your stroke and make an extended follow-through. Hitting fully through will send the ball running nicely over any rough spots in the hillock and then on to the hole."

Lee Trevino, *Groove Your Swing My Way*:
"Whenever you're just a foot or two off the green in a good lie, with short smooth grass leading up to the putting surface, your safest shot is to putt the ball."

CHAPTER 6

Practice, Practice, Practice

PROPER PRACTICE

The average Weekend Golfer typically practices only on the day he plans to play golf. Practice between rounds is not routine and is usually done only when a special golfing event is planned. Practice after a round or in other places such as at home or in the office is often not even considered. The average golfer is too busy for practice. He only wants to *play* golf. He doesn't want to bother with practicing.

> **PRACTICE LETS YOU BUILD AND REFINE YOUR STROKE.**

In *Natural Golf*, Seve Ballesteros writes, "Unfortunately, practice never makes you perfect at golf, but practice is indispensable because it is the only way to be fully prepared for the challenges and opportunities with which the course will present you each time you play." Continuing, Seve says, "No amount of practice will ever groom anyone to play golf to absolute perfection. But, because proper practice trains you to hit all sorts of shots and builds confidence, it prepares you for the endless challenges involved in playing to your best potential."

Practice develops muscle memory, skill, confidence, and a positive mental approach. But only if you practice properly, with a purpose in mind, can you become a better all-around golfer. As the saying goes, "Practice makes perfect." But only if it's correct practice. Keep this in mind when deciding how much time you want to devote to practicing. You'll be given practice guidelines later in this chapter.

Practice is important no matter how little time you devote to it. Once you understand the basics, you'll learn that the quality of practice is more important than the amount of practice. You can then practice less than other golfers.

PRACTICE SESSIONS

Practice can be done anytime, anywhere—it doesn't have to be on a golf course, or at a driving range. It could be at home, in an office, at a park, or in a field. It could be anywhere! Work with a purpose in mind during every practice round. Don't just go out to the driving range, or practice putting green, and hit ball after ball without thought or plan. Just hitting ball after ball will produce no obvious benefits. You wouldn't hit like that on the golf course, so why practice that way? There are many ways to practice, depending on how and when you do it.

1. PRACTICE BEFORE A ROUND. For those of you who can only find time to practice just before a round, plan to spend at least 40 minutes before your tee-off time. Make a deliberate choice. Choose an interval of practice time and stick to it every time you play. When practicing before a round, you should work on both putting and swinging your woods and irons. As an average Weekend Golfer, you should spend more time on putting. And if time is short, practice *only* putting.

Most golfers will head directly for the driving range to practice their woods and irons and then end up on the putting green. Even though putting may seem less exciting than hitting balls into the air, putting practice is actually more important to the game of the average Weekend Golfer.

> PUTTING IS THE ONE AREA OF
> GOLF IN WHICH YOU CAN EXCEL
> AND ACHIEVE PUTTING SCORES
> EQUAL TO A GOLF PRO.

Practice putting first. It'll take a deliberate effort to change your habits. But you must try. Going to the putting green first will develop your rhythm and confidence, two elements needed in all parts of your game. Techniques for practicing on the putting green follow in the next few pages. How you practice on the driving range is your choice.

A. Constantly Check Body and Club Position. Check the squareness of your stance and putterhead alignment in relation to the line of putt, the correctness of your grip, and be sure your putter lies flat on the green. Practice ball alignment and take several backstrokes and forward strokes to get a rhythm. Use the manufacturer's name on the ball to help line up the putt.

Practice plumb-bobbing on several putts. Because it takes extra time to set up this way, you don't have to practice plumb-bobbing on every putt during practice—unless of course you haven't mastered your plumb-bobbing techniques. When beginning your practice session, your main goal is to position yourself correctly. You can worry about more precise aiming when on the course. Work on getting close to the hole no matter how short the putt.

B. Work on Short Putts First. Your first putt should be a short one from about 2 feet from the hole. Set up balls around the hole and step up to each as if you were about to make an important putt on the course. Don't forget to aim at a spot along the line of putt, not the hole. Make a succession of these short putts. If you are missing short putts, take a little more time before stroking the ball—don't rush your stroke. A slight movement of the head can twist your putterface out of alignment and a missed putt will be the result. Try moving even closer to the hole. If your ball is still missing the hole, try putting from 6 inches. If you're still not sinking the ball in the dead center of the hole, turn your putterface right or left,

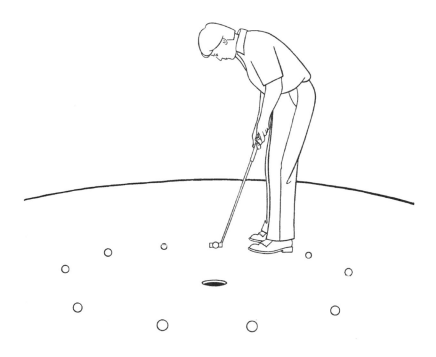

Figure 33. Practice Short Putt

until the putterface is at right angles to the line of putt. Now move back by 1-foot increments and try to sink the ball. Don't change your distance until you've sunk a succession of shots at a given distance.

Making these short putts will give you confidence to move back to longer distances. Next try 6 feet and hit 10 more shots. Keep in mind that you cannot make every putt, no matter how good you are. Once you're comfortable with a set distance and can make most of those shots, move progressively farther back. As you get farther away, your goal should be to get the ball in close to the hole rather than to hole out. Don't forget to use a 3-foot imaginary target and aim for the *pro* side on these longer putts. Continue moving back by 10-foot increments, but don't spend too much time on putts over 40 feet. Making a putt that long is pure luck and you're not likely to be faced with many of them during a round.

Practice short, long, and straight putts for at least 75 percent of the time you have allotted yourself to putting practice. If you're lucky, the practice green will be hilly and you can spend the remaining 25 percent of your time practicing uphill, downhill, and sidehill putts. Evaluate how grain affects your ball. This will help you to determine how hard a stroke is needed when the ball is moving with, against, or across the grain. Whatever you do, don't practice the same shot over and over. Change ball position constantly. Simulate a variety of course conditions.

C. Putting Exceptionally Well in Practice. Be extra careful if you're putting exceptionally well on the practice green. Don't be fooled into thinking you can't miss. Many times I've putted well in practice but found I couldn't duplicate those skills on the course. I had become overconfident and failed to analyze why I was putting so well in practice.

No matter how well you think you're putting, you're still an average Weekend Golfer.

If you're putting much better than usual, step back and figure out why. You've probably gotten it all together just for the moment, but it isn't likely to last throughout the entire round. If you are putting well, enjoy it, but don't cut short the time you've allotted to practice.

D. Two or More Practice Greens. Sometimes a course will have two or more practice putting greens. It's important that you *only* practice on the green that's close in type and texture to the greens on the course. Otherwise, your game could suffer as a result.

> **YOUR OBJECTIVE IS TO DUPLICATE
> PLAYING CONDITIONS AS
> CLOSELY AS POSSIBLE DURING
> YOUR PRACTICE SESSIONS.**

Ask the starter, or those just finishing their round, which practice putting green is closest in texture and grass type to the greens on the course. If you do not get a satisfactory answer, walk to a nearby green and see for yourself. But don't touch or play on the green. It's against the rules of golf to test a course green before play.

I know of one course in Southern California with two practice greens. One green is quite flat, typically cut short, and closely represents the greens on the course. The other green is well-watered, lush, and two-tiered. It's a much nicer green and is more fun to putt on. But, while you can practice severe breaking putts and steep uphill, downhill, and sidehill putts on this green, it's not anything like the greens on the course. You'll have fun but you'll just be wasting your pre-round practice time. I don't suggest practicing on a green that is different from those on the course. You may want to practice between rounds on such a putting green, but it won't be helpful to use it just before a round.

2. PRACTICE BETWEEN ROUNDS. While the basics should be practiced just prior to a round, *between rounds* concentrate on your weaknesses, changes in putting style, new putters, and techniques designed to help you become a better putter. Plan to practice for at least 45 minutes—30 on putting, and 15 on woods and irons. Or you may want to devote an entire practice session just to putting. Take this book with you when you practice. Select a chapter and work on it. Each time you practice, start by working on familiar points and finish by working on new ones. Over time you'll cover all of the points outlined.

Take a writing pad to each practice session and make notes on those areas you're good at and those that need further practice.

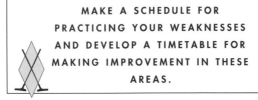

MAKE A SCHEDULE FOR
PRACTICING YOUR WEAKNESSES
AND DEVELOP A TIMETABLE FOR
MAKING IMPROVEMENT IN THESE
AREAS.

Keep these notes with you whenever you play golf and refer to them often. There's a lot to learn and it's easy to forget.

In addition to developing the details of your putting style in these between-round practice sessions, pay particular attention to using an imaginary target, stroking the putter smoothly, keeping your head still, and putting from off the green. A proper way to practice each of these important areas follows:

A. Imaginary 3-foot Target. Work on long putts using an imaginary 3-foot diameter target. An easy way to visualize this target area is to place tees 1½ feet to the left and right of the hole with the hole in the middle. First try lagging two or three balls into the target area from 10 feet away and then move to 20 feet, then to 30 feet, and so forth, until you can roll the ball into the target area from any distance almost every time. Your main object during practice is to lag into the target area—not sink the ball! When you've had a reasonable amount of success, you can work on aiming for the *pro* side of the hole, while at the same time, trying to place your ball closer to the hole.

B. Keeping Your Head Still. When putting, you often have an overwhelming tendency to lift your head to see where your ball is going. Try putting with your eyes closed. This is an excellent technique for keeping your head still until after impact. It will control the temptation to watch the ball and to pull the putterhead off line in your forward stroke. It will also help you to hit the ball in a smooth, fluid manner. It will help to lessen your anxiety on future putts of all lengths. Try hitting a series of shots with your eyes closed. Make sure that no one is nearby, so you won't interfere with others who are practicing on the same green.

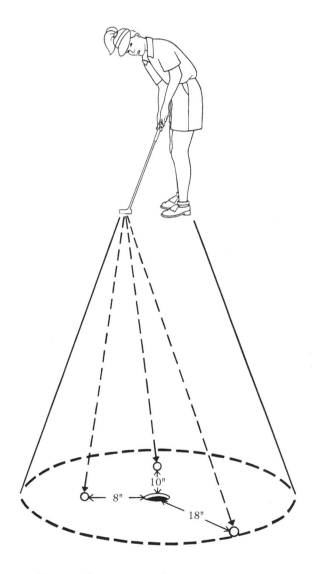

Figure 34. Practice with an Imaginary Target

C. Stroking the Putter Smoothly. There are several methods for learning to use a smooth stroke when putting. The one I prefer is called the *two-club technique*. Begin your setup by selecting a target about 10 feet away. While the hole is the obvious target, you can choose to aim at an arbitrary target, such as a tee stuck into the ground, a coin, or a dark spot on the green.

Place two clubs lengthwise on the green, about 6 inches apart, and parallel to each other with the toes of the clubs facing outward. Position the clubs so they form an alley to the target. The center of the alley should be aligned with the center of the target. You may have to stand 10 feet behind the clubs to make sure the centers are aligned and that the clubs are parallel to each other. Place a ball in the center of the two clubs and putt your ball down the alley toward the target. By keeping your putterhead within the area defined by the two clubs, you can develop a smooth, straight backstroke and forward stroke. The two clubs will keep you honest. If your stroke should stray from the alley formed by the two clubs, your putterhead, or ball, may strike one of the two clubs lying on the ground. Your objective is to stroke your putter smoothly so you can propel the ball forward in an accelerating, even tempo, without touching either of the two clubs.

Visualize your putter starting from the dead center of the two clubs and your ball traveling straight down the middle toward the target, without wobbling to one side or the other. Work on a smooth backstroke and forward stroke. Keep your head still and always aim for your target. You might even try closing your eyes. As your abilities improve try placing the clubs closer together.

D. Putting from Off the Green. Once you have established your new putting style, putting from off the green will be easy to learn. You just need experience. Try putting from the fringe, from 6 inches away, from 3 feet, and from as far back as you choose. Experiment with different lies such as hard grass, heavy grass, wet grass, or bare ground. If you can find a putting green that's hilly, try putting up to the green one time and down to the green the next. See how much more secure you have to be in your stance and how much harder you have to hit a ball for it to travel through grass. Try to

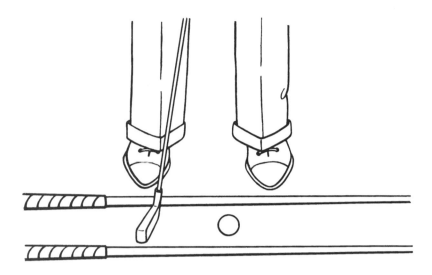

Figure 35. Two-Club Stroking Technique

develop some consistency in your strokes whether short or long, then make adjustments to help control the force of your strokes.

3. PRACTICE AFTER A ROUND. A practice period after a round is the best time to correct mistakes but many golfers have never even considered practicing after a round! Many golf pros practice soon after a round. They know what has been bothering them on the course and they know that the best time to correct those problems is immediately after a round while the problems are clearly remembered. Give it a try—at least once. You might find this new practice time very helpful to your overall game. It can reinforce your confidence and give you motivation to play another round.

4. OTHER PRACTICE. You can really practice almost anywhere, any time you want to. It can be done indoors or outdoors, any place you have room. You can start and stop when you want to. You could

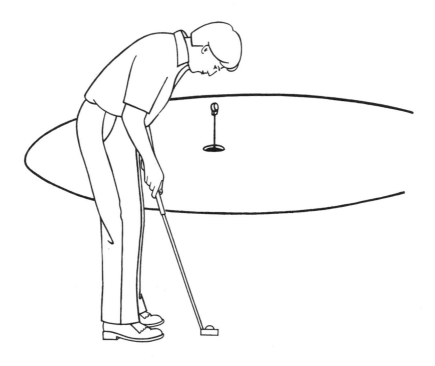

Figure 36. Practice Putting from Off the Green

take your putter along on trips and practice putting in a hotel or motel room. You could practice putting at your work place in an office or on a lawn during a break period.

AT HOME YOU COULD TRY:

A. Taking your stance in front of a mirror and comparing your poses with the illustrations in this book.

B. Gripping and regripping your putter.

C. Putting on a rug into a glass.

D.   Stroking the putter backward and forward in a smooth and fluid manner, with or without the *two-club technique.*

There is much you can to do to improve, or maintain, your putting skills away from the golf course between rounds, or during very hot or very cold weather when golf is not practical for the average golfer. You can watch golf on television, read golf books and magazines, and you could even make a videotape of yourself and analyze your own game in the comfort of your home. The more exposure you have to golf in general, the greater the chance you'll increase your playing confidence. And many golf pros will tell you that confidence is the overriding factor in winning golf.

PRACTICE—IF ONLY TO WARM UP YOUR MUSCLES

Have you ever heard someone say, "I cannot practice before a round, it makes me tired?"

> PRACTICE IS NOT ONLY A WAY TO
> REINFORCE YOUR GOLFING
> SKILLS, IT'S ALSO AN EFFECTIVE
> MEANS OF WARMING THE
> MUSCLES YOU'LL BE USING ON
> THE COURSE.

How many times have you gone out on a course and played poorly for the first two or three holes, only to show remarkable improvement as the game progressed? You improved because your muscles had time to warm up, resulting in a better game and increased confidence.

Just think what your game could be like if you warm up before going to the first tee. Getting your muscles ready for golf is especially important if you don't play or practice often. A proper warm-up prevents many aches and pains and improves your rhythm during pre-round practice. So practice—if only to warm up your muscles.

If you absolutely hate practice but still want to go out and enjoy the game, at least practice aiming and setting up with your woods, irons, and putter at home. While you probably can't hit any balls with your woods and irons, you can stroke 10 short and 10 long putts on a carpet before going out to play. This will produce some rhythm and balance and will help to warm up your muscles. It will also help to put you in the mood to play golf. You'll now be able to play better than if you had no practice at all.

TIME REQUIRED TO PRACTICE YOUR NEW TECHNIQUES

Practice time is a personal choice but do yourself a favor and allot specific times to practice sessions. You'll have to practice more intently at first. Practice often at home, between rounds, just prior to a round, and even after a round. Allow at least 45 minutes for any practice session until your putting abilities improve. You may not like it, but at least for a while you have to practice as much as you can to develop your new putting style and to become accustomed to the new techniques presented in this book. Even if your practice doesn't involve using a ball, just picking up your putter and stroking it 10 or 12 times a day will help.

Set a regular routine for practicing golf at home, between rounds, and after a round. Allow extra time for practicing new techniques. At home, you may want to practice putting into a glass for 10 minutes, three times a week. Perhaps you could spend 15 minutes a day on both Saturday and Sunday swinging your woods and irons. Keep a putter in your closet at home or in your office and practice whenever you have the chance.

Have fun, be competitive, and practice often. It will pay off in the long run. It's often difficult to practice new techniques while competing with your friends, so you may want to practice these new techniques alone. You'll probably have an adjustment period in which your game will suffer for a brief period. In a fairly short time, your game will improve and you'll be a much better player.

**HOW YOU IMPROVED
"OVERNIGHT" CAN BE
YOUR SECRET.**

Arrange a golfing schedule that allows you to practice aiming one week, setting up to a putt the next, stroking the ball the next week, and putting from off the green the next. You may want to devote more time to your weaknesses. Whatever you do, be sure to keep track of your current scores and compare them with your scores in six months. You'll be pleasantly surprised. Remember to separate the total number of strokes taken with the putter on the green from those taken with woods and irons.

CHAPTER 7

Putting Etiquette and Rules You Ought to Know

ETIQUETTE IS OFTEN TAKEN FOR GRANTED

If you know how to play golf you know how to behave on the golf course. Nothing is further from the truth. Few average Weekend Golfers know much about golf etiquette.

> **PUT SIMPLY, GOLF ETIQUETTE IS COMMON COURTESY ON A GOLF COURSE.**

It's how we expect others to act. Actually, etiquette is a difficult concept for golfers of all experience levels. If you tell them they have poor manners on the course, they'll be offended. It can be a touchy subject. Based on my research, I think that you have to be taught good behavior on the golf course—it just doesn't come naturally. Read on and learn the basics of good golf etiquette.

We've all seen golfers who think they own the course, are deliberately rude, just don't care about others' property, or perhaps don't know any better. These same golfers sometimes have temper tantrums and throw clubs or break them in half. They'll curse continually—at themselves, at other golfers, at the golf course, and even at that tiny defenseless ball. This behavior clearly demonstrates an ignorance of proper etiquette, a bad attitude, or poor sportsmanship.

It can be frustrating to seasoned golfers to play with those who don't understand golfing etiquette or the rules of golf. Uninformed golfers will walk onto a green and drop their golf bag on its surface. They will forget to bring the putter onto the green. They'll carelessly walk to their ball while tromping all over other players' lines of putt. If they mark their ball at all, they will often pick up the ball first before placing a marker down in its place. They'll talk while others are setting up shots or will stand directly behind the golfer who is about to putt. They'll rarely hole out a short putt. When adding up their score, they'll conveniently forget a few strokes or won't add penalty strokes incurred. Their attitude on and off the green does not make for a pleasant round of golf for any one of the golfers playing with this rude person.

Unfortunately, this absence of proper behavior is not restricted to just the uninformed. Etiquette is rarely taught because, if you play golf, you are expected to know golfing etiquette. That's why golf etiquette is taken for granted. There are few golfers who know or practice good golfing etiquette. There are books that teach etiquette, but *you* must make an effort to read those books and apply what you learn. So make the effort and read on. You and those you play with will be glad you did.

BASIC GOLFING ETIQUETTE

Using good manners in golf can make the game more enjoyable for everyone. While some of these manners seem obvious, they are often taken for granted, and therefore must be reinforced from time to time. There is a fine line between golfing etiquette and the rules of golf, so pay particular attention to those manners and rules that, if violated, could result in penalty strokes.

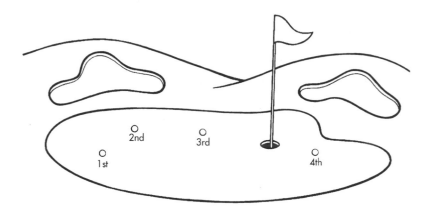

Figure 37. First Person to Putt

The proper mind set for putting on or off the green can be achieved by observing the basic rules of good manners as noted in the following pages. If you can apply these rules to your game, you will have the makings of a well-mannered golfer.

THE MIND SET OF GOOD ETIQUETTE

1. When approaching the green, place your golf bag just off the fringe or in an area designated for golf clubs. Take your putter and walk directly toward your ball, being careful not to walk through other players' lines of putt. The player whose ball is farthest from the hole typically will putt first. The next farthest putts second, and so on.

2. Never step in another player's line. Be careful how you walk on the green. Don't tear the surface with your spikes. Walk on the green the way you'd walk on an expensive carpet. Don't damage the putting green by leaning on your putter.

3. Carefully mark your ball by placing a marker, or small coin, behind your ball. Don't be sloppy about marking it. Don't pick up

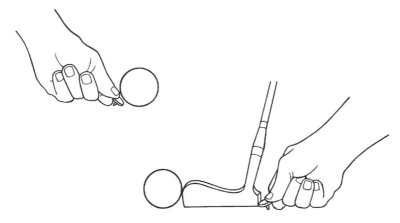

Figure 38. Marking Ball's Position

your ball until you've properly marked it. Then pick the ball up and keep it with you until it's your turn to putt. Don't throw it back on the green. While it's in your possession, it's a good idea to clean it—a clean ball will roll smoother on the green. Always place the marker behind the ball so that the ball is between the marker and hole.

4. If a ball marker interferes with the line of putt, stance, or stroke of another player, the marker should be placed one or more putterhead lengths to one side. When it's your turn to putt, don't forget to replace the ball in its original position. Some players mark in front of the ball and then when replacing the ball will move the ball in front of the marker—this is like stealing two inches closer to the hole. So watch your opponents. Keep them honest.

5. While no one else is putting, repair any ball mark you notice. You can repair an old hole plug or damage to the green caused by the impact of a ball, whether or not your ball lies on the green. *But* you cannot repair spike marks, damage to the cup area, or any other damage to the green until everyone in your group has holed out.

6. While many players remove the flag stick when arriving on the green, it's actually more courteous to leave it in the hole and let the

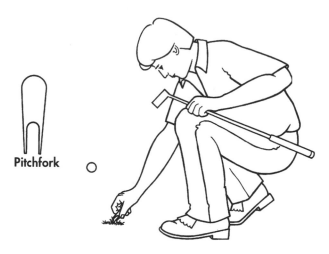

Pitchfork

Ball marks on putting greens may be repaired even if they're on your line. As a matter of fact, they should be repaired, no matter where they are. Use a tee or pitchfork repairer to loosen the soil around the ball mark. Then pull the turf toward the center of the damaged spot. The smoothing process can be done either with a putter, one's hand, or by stepping down on the spot.

Figure 39. Repairing Ball Mark on Green

first player to putt make the decision to remove it. He has the right to have someone hold the flag stick while he's putting. If this first player doesn't think he needs the flag stick, then he should ask the rest of the group if it's okay to take the flag stick out of the hole and lay it away from the balls still on the green. The farther you are from the flag stick, the more likely you'll want to have it held for you—it serves as a good visual guide to the location of that tiny hole. Any player has the right to have the flag stick held in place when it's that player's turn even if it has already been removed and put aside.

7.   Be quiet. It's the Golden Rule of golf. When it's your turn to set up to putt, you expect others to be quiet—and they expect the same of you.

8. When it's not your turn, don't talk or walk around the green for any reason. Be careful where you stand while others are putting. Stand away from the player who is putting—keep out of his line of vision. Don't cast a shadow on another player's ball, or on the line of putt. If you notice your shadow is interfering, step back.

9. Wait until the other player's ball has completely stopped before addressing your own ball if your turn is next. Similarly, the player putting must wait for his ball to stop completely before taking further action.

10. If the player putting asks you to hold the flag stick while he's putting, be sure to lift it straight up and hold it in a vertical position. Grab the flag stick by the flag and hold it tight—a flapping flag can be distracting. If the ball is headed for the hole, remove the flag stick and step away before the ball reaches the hole. If the ball hits you or the flag stick, the player putting will be subject to a two-stroke penalty. While holding the flag stick, be careful not to walk close to the hole or step on other players' line of putt. You might leave spike marks that could affect the roll of the ball.

11. When it's your turn to putt, replace your original ball on the green and pick up your marker. You can't use a different ball unless your original ball is damaged and is unplayable; in which case, you must announce to your opponents that you'll be using a different ball. Watch this one: many golfers use one ball on the course and another on the green.

12. Don't delay. Be prompt about taking aim, setting up, and stroking the ball. If your ball goes into the hole, quickly go to the hole and pick it up. Don't leave it in the hole. If your ball does not go in, mark it, pick it up, and wait for your next turn.

13. Sometimes you'll hit your ball too far and you'll still be the farthest away. In this case, you do not lose your turn. Be gracious. Mark the ball, pick it up, clean it, and replace it on the green. Take aim, set up, and promptly stroke it.

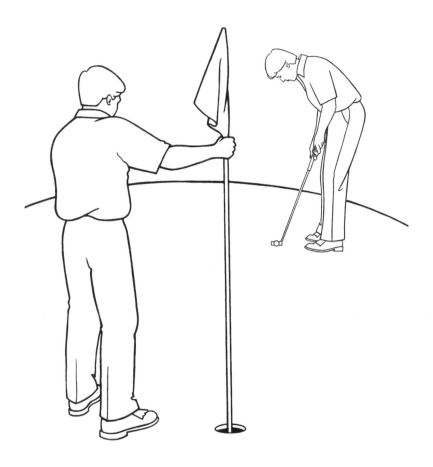

Figure 40. Holding Flag Stick for Another Player

14. Putt out no matter how short the putt. Some golfers will pick up their ball if they are within a foot of the hole. In most games, this is not legal. In friendly games, you may want to establish guidelines for these *gimmes*. At the start of the game, establish how far away a player can be from the hole to pick it up. In essence, you are saying to the player, "Why bother putting, we know you can make that short putt." But *don't* pick up your ball unless you have established beforehand that your group will be accepting *gimmes*. It can be very annoying if someone just picks up his ball for no apparent reason.

In reality, the short putt is perhaps one of the most difficult shots in the game of golf and everyone should putt out. It's assumed that anyone can make a putt of a foot or less but this is simply not the case. Golf pros have been known to lose major tournaments for missing putts as short as 3 inches!

1 5. Don't discuss your putt until everyone in your group has finished. After putting don't say, "This green is faster than it looks" or "Did you see that break?" These statements could be more confusing than helpful. Wait until everyone has finished putting before making comments.

1 6. Wait for everyone in your group to hole out before leaving the green. It isn't polite to march off to the next tee without waiting to observe how the rest of your golf group did.

1 7. When the last player has holed out, replace the flag stick in the hole and make sure it's vertical. It can be annoying to those approaching the green if the flag stick is crooked, or even missing.

1 8. Leave the green as a group. Go to your golf bag and put your putter away. Take out your scorecard and mark your score plus any penalty strokes incurred.

1 9. Occasionally, you may want to replay (as practice only) a missed putt. This is permissible provided everyone in your group has holed out and that you're not holding up play for your own group or for anyone approaching the green. In general, retrying a putt is not good practice. In any case, *don't* retry a putt until everyone in your group has holed out.

2 0. Compliment other players regardless of whether they are opponents or partners. If a player has made a good attempt at a long putt, has made a tricky downhill putt, or has just made a one-putt from any distance, it deserves a pleasant remark. It is, of course, not acceptable to tell him that he made a lousy shot or to make some other rude comment. Be careful about complimenting someone who doesn't take criticism well. You may think he made a great shot but *he* may not agree. And if you compliment him, he may become upset. If you sense that he doesn't handle compliments well—just refrain from any comment. You don't need enemies when playing golf.

21. Watch your tongue and your body language. One upset golfer can ruin the day for everyone in the group.

YOU'RE SUPPOSED TO KNOW THE RULES

How do golfers learn the rules of golf, or the rules of any sport? They typically learn from their friends. And where do their friends learn? From other friends. From television. From just playing. They rarely pick up a copy of the rules and read it from cover to cover.

But do they really know the rules? No. They usually know the most obvious ones and those that have benefited them the most in the past. And they're certainly not eager to apply penalty strokes to their score. The average Weekend Golfer does not really know the rules of golf as they apply to the green. He doesn't know he can't give advice to others, test the surface of the green with his hand, or how long he can wait before a lingering ball falls into a hole. Many, I am sure, would rather forego the rules and play any way they please. They think rules are a burden and make the game more difficult.

Golf is a serious game with many rules. Some of the more basic ones used on or around the green are summarized in the next few pages. As indicated in the Notes section at the beginning of the book, these rules may vary depending on whether you're participating in match or stroke play. Keep this in mind.

The rules listed below are just reminders of the more important ones to understand and use. The penalty for violation of any rule of golf is two-strokes, unless otherwise stated. Refer to the *USGA's Rules of Golf in Pictures* for complete details and penalties that must be applied in specific situations. The rules do vary according to whether you're playing match or stroke play and they can even vary based on local rulings. Do yourself a favor and ask the starter before playing a round of golf of the basic rules that are applicable to this particular golf course. The more important rules follow:

SUMMARY OF PUTTING RULES OF GOLF

1. ADVICE. Generally, a player cannot ask for any counsel or suggestions which could influence his play, choice of club, or method of making a stroke. Questions about the rules of golf or the position of hazards or location of the flag stick on the green are not considered advice.

2. REPAIR OF HOLE PLUGS, BALL MARKS, AND OTHER DAMAGE. A player may not repair damage to the putting green, other than hole plugs or ball marks, that assist the player in his subsequent play of the hole. Damage to the putting green caused by golf shoe spikes should be repaired on completion of the hole.

3. USING A DIFFERENT BALL WHEN PUTTING. A player may not use a different ball when putting unless he has announced to his opponents that his ball is unfit for play; in which case, the others in his group must agree with the decision to replace the original ball with a different ball. If he violates this rule, he shall incur a one-stroke penalty.

4. HITTING TO THE WRONG GREEN. If a ball accidentally lands on the wrong green, the ball must be picked up and dropped off that green within one club length nearest to where the ball lies on the wrong green, no closer to the correct green. In determining where to drop the ball off the green, the player may not drop it into a hazard or back onto the wrong putting green.

5. LINE OF PUTT. Another player may suggest a line of putt, but if he touches the putting green with his club to indicate such, he is subject to a two-stroke penalty. Also, a mark may not be placed on the green to give a visual bearing for the ball's path.

6. CASUAL WATER ON THE GREEN. If there is a puddle of water on the green between a ball and the flag stick, the ball may be picked up and moved to a point where there is a clear line of putt away from the casual water but no nearer to the hole. If a ball is off the green, it cannot be moved to avoid casual water. Dew and frost are not casual water.

7. TESTING SURFACE. During the play of a hole, a player shall not test the surface of the putting green by rolling a ball across it or roughening or scraping the surface with a shoe, club, hand, or ball because it can give him an unfair advantage regarding grain, grass height and type, and slope.

8. USING AN ARTIFICIAL MEASURING DEVICE OR OTHER UN-USUAL EQUIPMENT. Generally, a player may not use any artificial devices or equipment for the purpose of gauging, measuring distance or judging conditions that may affect his play or assist in gripping a club. The penalty for using such a device is disqualification from play.

9. BALL INTERFERING WITH OR ASSISTING PLAY. Any player may lift his ball if he considers that his ball might assist another player. He can also have any other ball lifted if he considers that the ball might interfere with his play or assist the play of any other player. In either case, the ball cannot be touched while another ball is in motion.

10. NOT MARKING A BALL BEFORE LIFTING. A ball must be properly marked with either a ball-marker or a small coin. Picking up a ball without accurately marking its position is illegal and subject to a one-stroke penalty. Marking ball position with a tee is illegal. The position of a ball to be lifted should be marked by placing a ball-marker, a small coin, or other similar object immediately behind the ball. If a ball-marker interferes with the play, stance, or stroke of another player, it should be placed one or more putterhead lengths to one side.

11. SOMEONE ELSE MARKS YOUR BALL. Typically, the golfer closest to a ball that is interfering with another golfer's line of putt should mark the position of that ball, whether or not it's his ball. When it's the turn of the player who owns the ball just marked, the person originally marking the ball shall replace the ball for the owner. The owner of the ball shall not replace his own ball *if* he did not mark it himself.

12. MOVING A BALL OR MARKER. If a ball or marker is accidentally moved while picking up a ball, or removing a loose impediment, either can be replaced without penalty provided the marker was put down behind the ball before it was picked up.

13. BALL LYING NEXT TO FLAG STICK. If the ball is wedged between the flag stick and the hole, the flag stick must be lifted straight up and out. If the ball stays in the hole, it counts as a completed stroke. If the ball pops out, it must be replaced on the lip of the hole and cannot be counted as a completed stroke.

14. BALL OVERHANGING LIP OF HOLE. If the ball is hanging over the edge of the hole, the player can walk to it and wait another 10 seconds for it to drop. If the ball drops after the time period, it will be considered holed out but the player will incur a one-stroke penalty.

15. FLAG STICK ATTENDED, REMOVED, OR HELD UP. Before stroking the ball, the player may have the flag stick attended, removed, or held up to indicate the position of the hole. This may only be done on the authority of the player before he plays his stroke. The player holding the flag stick may either stand nearby or hold the flag stick in place. If the player who is putting does not ask anyone to hold the flag stick and his ball is headed for the hole, another player cannot rush over and remove the flag stick. If the player putting hits the flag stick because he neglected to authorize someone to hold the flag stick, he will incur a two-stroke penalty.

16. BALL STRIKES FLAG STICK. If a putted ball on the green strikes a flag stick which is in the hole, is being held, or has been removed and placed flat on the putting surface away from the lines of putt, the player striking the flag stick is subject to a two-stroke penalty.

17. BALL STRIKES ANOTHER BALL ON PUTTING SURFACE. If a ball at rest is struck and moved by another ball, it must be replaced in its original position without penalty. If the player who hit the ball at rest is also on the green, then he shall incur a two-stroke penalty. If a player is off the green and strikes another player's ball on the green, the ball on the green at rest shall be replaced in its original position. The player who hit the ball at rest from off the green must leave his own ball where it landed but incurs no penalty.

18. STANDING ASTRIDE OR ON LINE OF PUTT. A player shall not make a stroke on the green from a stance astride, or with either foot touching the line of putt, or an extension of that line behind the ball.

19. PRACTICE. A player shall not practice a stroke either during the play of a hole or between the play of two holes except that, between the play of two holes, the player may practice putting or chipping on or near the putting green of the hole last played. He may also practice on a practice putting green or the teeing area of the next hole to be played in the round, provided such practice strokes are not played from a hazard and do not unduly delay play. Practice swings may be taken at any place, provided the player does not violate the rules of golf.

You'll find that there are other rules of golf but that these are the more common ones encountered during a typical round of golf.

CHAPTER 8

Getting It All Together

START LEARNING NOW

When you're finished reading this book, go out to a local golf course and start practicing. Or go to an open area like a park, a field, or start practicing in your own home. But whatever you do—*start*. Begin right away working on your new putting style. Compare your current putting style with the one I recommend in this book. Check your grip, stance, setup, aim, eyes and head position, flatness of the putter sole, and how you stroke the ball. Practice taking your stance and basic club position in front of a mirror. Look at the illustrations in this book and compare your poses with the pictures.

DON'T MIX OLD AND NEW PUTTING STYLES

Practice this new putting style before playing a round. If you go out for a round before perfecting the new strokes, use them anyway. Don't worry if your scores are high. They will get better soon. No matter how difficult or awkward the new style seems at first, keep at it. By all means, don't revert to using your old putting style—you will then spoil all that you have studied so hard to accomplish. Don't give up too soon: keep trying. If a technique doesn't seem to work for you, read the text again and make sure you're following the instructions. Keep at it. Give yourself time—your putting *will* improve and you'll be glad you were patient. Persistence pays off. Good things happen to those who wait.

DEVELOP A PUTTING ROUTINE

Each time you play a new hole, you must follow a set routine when you get near the green.

> YOUR APPROACH TO THE GREEN,
> THE WAY YOU PUTT, THE WAY
> YOU PICK UP YOUR BALL, AND
> THE WAY YOU LEAVE THE
> GREEN SHOULD BE THE SAME
> EVERY TIME.

Approaching the green, evaluating your lie, marking and cleaning your ball, aiming, gripping your putter, setting up, aligning the putterface with the ball, positioning your head over the ball, and stroking the ball must become natural. This is your putting routine. Your putting style is an integral part of your putting routine. In some cases, you may even think that your putting style *is* your putting routine.

Write down your present routine and then study the suggested routine that follows. This putting routine is a combination of good strategy, sound technique, basic etiquette, common sense, and the rules of golf. Compare your routine with the one suggested in this book. Add what you think is necessary to make your own routine complete or just use mine. But whatever you do, use a predetermined routine when approaching, putting, and leaving a green. It *will* make a difference.

STEPS REQUIRED IN PUTTING ROUTINE

1. Examine the basic layout of the green as you approach it.

2. Upon reaching the green, set your clubs down off the green, take your putter, walk toward your ball, and survey your line of putt by walking around the ball and observing its lie from all angles. By doing this, you will be able to see if your line of putt is going uphill, downhill, or flat. This simple survey will save you many strokes.

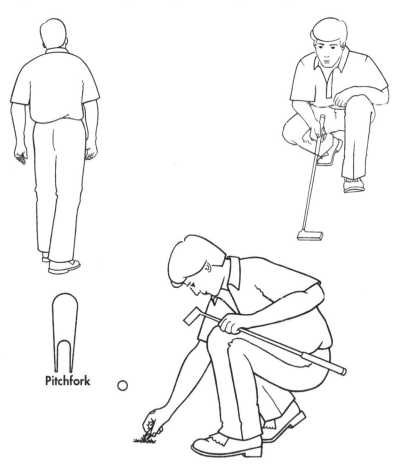

Pitchfork

Figure 41. Steps Required in Putting Routine

3. While on the green, repair any ball marks you see. Use a wooden tee, or a tool called a *pitchfork*, to repair those ball marks. Lift the damaged turf with the tee or tool, level off the area by tapping the turf lightly with the sole of the putter. Your object is to make the damaged grass level with the rest of the green. Remember that ball marks left unrepaired not only spoil the game for others, but vastly increase the cost of maintaining a green.

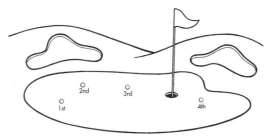

Figure 41a. Order of Play

4. Determine the order of play. This is typically a group decision. Generally, the player whose ball is farthest from the hole putts first. The next farthest away putts second and so forth. These rules change only when one player putts a ball in such a way as to be farther away from the hole than the player who was supposed to putt next. In other words, he doesn't lose his turn.

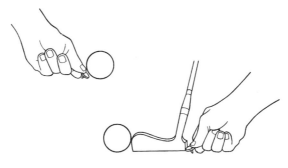

Figure 41b. Marking a Ball

5. Upon reaching your ball, mark your ball with a ball-marker or small coin by placing the marker behind the ball. Once marked, pick up your ball and clean it. Do not replace your ball until it's your turn to putt.

6. If you're not first to putt, observe how the other players' balls roll. Notice how hard they strike the ball, and whether the ball rolls more or less than you anticipated. Take advantage of every opportunity to study other players' results. Be a sound strategist. Stay alert to what is going on around you and try to profit from it. Analyze situations and try to turn them to your advantage.

7. When it's your turn, put your ball back on the green in front of your marker. Remove your marker.

8. Pace off the line between your ball and the hole to get an idea of actual distance and direction. Your putt may not be as long as it appears and the shot may be easier. If you *think* it's easier, it *will* be.

9. Don't dawdle, but don't hurry. Develop a positive plan. Every putt must be analyzed no matter how short. It can be infuriating to miss a 10-inch putt.

10. Determine your baseline.

Plumb-bobbing

Figure 41c. Aim by Plumb-bobbing

11. Determine your line of putt and break point by plumb-bobbing. Be careful that your break point takes into consideration the *pro* side of the hole. Study the slope of the green, the grain direction, grass height and type, and grass dampness. Remove any loose impediments along your line of putt.

Figure 41d. Align the Ball with the Heel of Left Foot

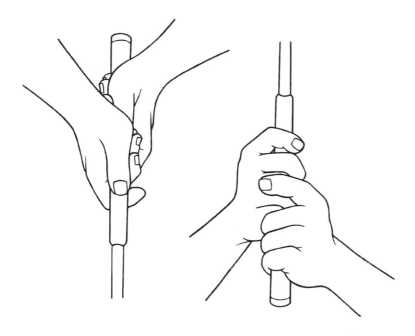

Figure 41e. Grip the Putter

1 2 .   On *a putt of one foot or more*, pick out a spot 6 to 8 inches from your ball along your line of putt. Take a balanced stance, grip the putter handle using the reverse-overlap grip, and align the ball with the putterface and with the heel of your left foot. Remember to position the putterhead at right angles to your line of putt. On *a putt of less than one foot*, pick out a spot just a few inches in front of your ball.

1 3 .   When taking your stance, be sure that the putter sole rests flat on the ground.

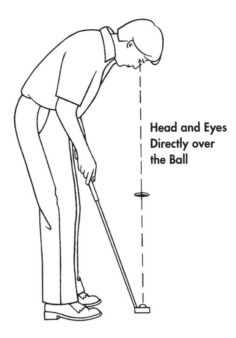

Head and Eyes
Directly over
the Ball

Figure 41f. Keep Head and Eyes Over the Ball

14. Keep your eyes directly over the ball and concentrate on hitting the back of the ball solidly.

15. Keep your head and body motionless.

16. Relax—mentally and physically.

17. When you're ready, you can make your stroke. If you don't want to take a practice stroke, continue to Step 20. Otherwise, go to Step 18 and take several practice strokes.

18. Step back about a foot and take a couple of practice strokes. You don't have to practice—but it's acceptable if you so desire. It's your choice. Be careful not to accidentally strike the ball during practice—it will count as a stroke!

19. When finally ready, move back into position. If you have any doubts about setup and aim when you have repositioned yourself, step back and perform your putting routine from Step 10. Don't cut short any step. This reevaluation step may be the reason why you choose not to take practice strokes just before taking a stroke. Without this reevaluation step, you may be just guessing that you can reposition yourself exactly as before you took that practice stroke.

20. Make your stroke using the arms-and-shoulders stroke. Keep the putterhead low to the ground. Don't change your mind in mid-stroke. If you have any doubts—*stop*. Indecision at this point will invariably lead to a poorly executed shot. If you do stop, return to Step 10 and start the evaluation step again.

> **A.** Make the stroke primarily with your shoulders and upper arms. Accelerate through the ball at impact. Aim for your selected imaginary "X" spot along the intended line of putt. On long putts, remember to aim for your imaginary 3-foot target area.

> **B.** Keep your head down and listen for the ball to drop. If the ball fails to drop in the hole, mark your ball, and wait for your next turn. Repeat the setup routine from Step 7. It's important that you follow the exact routine each time regardless of how close to the hole you may be.

> **C.** Don't rush to tap the ball in. Many golfers, including golf pros, have missed putts as short as 3 inches from the hole because they rushed. I have seen golfers concentrate intently on each putt from 20 feet or more but when faced with a 1-to 2-foot putt they set up to the ball and putt quickly. This hurried stroke can be a fatal mistake.

> If you feel you're being rushed by your partners, remember

it's your game too. When it's your turn, you've every right to take a reasonable amount of time to study your putt regardless of the distance to the hole. If the yips start, step back, take a few deep breaths, and reposition yourself to make the shot.

D. When the ball goes into the hole, remove it promptly. It's common courtesy to do so before anyone else putts. Don't talk to anyone until everyone has holed out.

21. When everyone has holed out, replace the flag stick in the hole and quickly leave the green. Put away your putter. Take out your scorecard and mark your score. Keep a separate tally of your putting scores for future reference.

22. Proceed to the next hole. Generally, the person with the lowest score on the last hole played will hit first. Play the hole. When near the green, start thinking about your putting routine. Get in the habit of using your putting routine every time you approach a green whether during a practice round or during competition.

> Now **I'm** finished. But **You're** just beginning. The most important thing to remember is that, as an average Weekend Golfer, you are playing a game. So enjoy yourself.

ABOUT THE AUTHOR

I am an average Weekend Golfer like you. I am not a golf pro and never will be. While a golf pro writes a book to fit the needs of all experience levels, this book is written for the average Weekend Golfer. Being a Weekend Golfer myself, I have empathy for you. I know what you are feeling, as you struggle with your putting game. This is why I wrote the book, to help you, the Weekend Golfer, improve your putting game and even your overall approach to the game of golf.

But I am more than just a golfer, I am also an author of a book *Business Policies and Procedures Handbook,* published by Prentice-Hall, Inc. devoted to teaching others how to write instructional manuals on improving one's business through the use of consistent and well-written policies and procedures (or rules, regulations, guidelines). As a writer of instructional type manuals for 25 years, coupled with my 30 years experience as a Weekend Golfer, it becomes obvious why I am the right author for this book. I have been able to successfully present the secrets behind putting in a very concise, well-illustrated book that is easy to read and comprehend for any golfer regardless of experience level.

I have not always been a Weekend Golfer. While I attended the University of California at Santa Barbara (UCSB) from 1968 to 1972, I used to golf every day and I was a scratch golfer. I knew that if I played intensely with a coach that I could become a golf pro. Instead I chose to pursue my career in business. I do know that what I am teaching you today is great material; I only wish that I had such a book when I was learning the game.

I currently work as a writer responsible for documenting and developing recommendations for improvements to the company operations. I have a Masters in Business (MBA) from the University of California at Los Angeles (UCLA). I have been writing manuals on how to improve processes for more than 25 years. I have published many articles in local business journals. Using this experience, coupled with my love for golf and success stories in putting, I have written what is in my opinion the *best book ever on the subject of putting*. Due to this book's excellent tips and illustrations, the book can be used by anyone on any golf course in the world.

I guarantee that everyone will find something that will help them improve their golf game. If you use the majority of guidelines presented in this book, you will become a great putter. But if you just want to use a few of the tips presented, you will still reduce your putting scores because just one of my tips will put some added consistency to your game. Read the book and impress your friends by improving overnight!

BIBLIOGRAPHY

Allen, Frank Kenyon, Dale Mead, Tom Lo Presti, and Barbara Romack. *The Golfer's Bible.* New York: Doubleday, 1989.

Ballesteros, Seve, with John Andrisani. *Natural Golf.* New York: Atheneum, 1988.

Ballingall, Peter. *Learn Golf in a Weekend.* New York: Alfred A. Knopf, 1991.

Bolt, Tommy, with William C. Griffith. *How to Keep Your Temper on the Golf Course.* New York: David McKay Company, Inc., 1969.

Coyne, John. *Better Golf.* Chicago: Follett Publishing Company, 1972.

Dobereiner, Peter. *Golf Explained, How to Take Advantage of the Rules.* Great Britain: Royal & Ancient Golf Club of St. Andrews, 1976.

Editors of Golf Digest. *All About Putting.* New York: Coward, McCann & Geoghegan (A Golf Digest Book), 1973.

Editors of Golf Magazine. *Tips from the Teaching Pros.* New York: Harper & Row, 1969.

Floyd, Ray, with Larry Dennis. *From 60 Yards in.* New York: Harper & Row, 1987.

Ford, Doug. *Getting Started in Golf.* New York: Simon & Schuster (Fireside), 1964.

Galvano, Phil. *Secrets of Accurate Putting and Chipping.* Englewood Cliffs, NJ: Prentice-Hall, Inc., 1957.

Garrity, John. *Sports Illustrated Putting, The Stroke-Saver's Guide.* New York: Time Inc., 1991.

Golf Magazine's Handbook of Golf Strategy, ed. Robert Scharff and eds. of *Golf Magazine,* New York: Harper & Row, 1977.

Green, Robert, and Brian Morgan. *Classic Holes.* New York: Prentice-Hall Press, 1989.

Grout, Jack, with Dick Aultman. *Let Me Teach You Golf As I Taught Jack Nicklaus.* New York: Atheneum/Smi, Macmillian Publishing Company, 1975.

Harrison, Mike. *The Official Guide to Jack Nicklaus Computer Golf.* North Carolina: Compute Books, 1990.

Hay, Alex. *The Handbook of Golf.* New Hampshire: Pelham Books Ltd., 1985.

Kite, Tom, and Larry Dennis. *How to Play Consistent Golf.* Connecticut: Golf Digest/Tennis, Inc., 1990.

McCleery, Peter. *Tips from the Tour.* New York: Pocket Books (A Golf Digest Book), 1986.

McCormick, Bill. *The Complete Beginner's Guide to Golf.* New York: Doubleday & Company, 1974.

McLean, Jim, with Larry Dennis. *Golf Digest's Book of Drills.* New York: Pocket Books (A Golf Digest Book), 1990.

Michael, Tom, and the Editors of *Golf Digest. Golf's Winning Stroke: Putting.* New York: Coward-McCann, 1967.

Mulvoy, Mark. *Sports Illustrated Golf, Play Like a Pro.* New York: Winner's Circle Books, 1988.

Nicklaus, Jack. *My 55 Ways to Lower Your Golf Score.* New York: Simon & Schuster, 1964.

Nicklaus, Jack, with Ken Bowden. *Jack Nicklaus' Lesson Tee.* New York: Simon & Schuster (Fireside), 1977.

Nicklaus, Jack, with Ken Bowden. *Jack Nicklaus' Playing Lessons.* New York: Simon & Schuster, 1981.

Norman, Greg, with George Peper. *Shark Attack*. New York: Simon & Schuster (Fireside), 1988.

Pace, Roy. *Target Golf*. Arizona: The Body Press, 1986.

Palmer, Arnold. *My Game & Yours*. New York: Simon & Schuster, 1983.

Palmer, Arnold, and Peter Dobereiner. *Arnold Palmer's Complete Book of Putting*. New York: Atheneum, 1986.

Pelz, Dave, with Nick Mastroni. *Putt Like the Pros*. New York: HarperPerennial, 1989.

Player, Gary. *Positive Golf*. New York: McGraw-Hill Book Company, 1967.

Player, Gary, with Desmond Tolhurst. *Golf Begins at 50*. New York: Simon & Schuster, 1988.

Rankin, Judy, with Michael Aronstein. *A Natural Way to Golf Power*. New York: Cornerstone Library, 1977.

Rodriguez, Chi Chi, with John Andrisani. *101 Super Shots*. New York: HarperPerennial, 1990.

Rosburg, Bob. *The Putter Book*. Connecticut: Golf Digest, 1963.

1992 Rules of Golf, as approved by the United States Golf Association and the Royal and Ancient Golf Club of St. Andrews, Scotland. Effective January 1, 1993. Printed in U.S.A.

Saunders, Vivien. *The Complete Book of Golf Practice*. London: Stanley Paul, 1988.

Scharff, Robert, and the Editors of *Golf Magazine*. *Golf Magazine's Encyclopedia of Golf*. New York: Harper & Row, 1966.

Smith, Horton, and Dawson Taylor. *The Secret of . . . Holing Putts!* New York: A. S. Barnes & Co., Inc., 1961.

Snead, Sam, and Jerry Tarde. *Pigeons, Marks, Hustlers*. Connecticut: A Golf Digest/Tennis, Inc., 1986.

Stanley, Louis T. *This is Putting.* London: W. H. Allen, 1968.

Stobbs, John. *The Anatomy of Golf.* New York: Emerson Books Inc., 1962.

Swarbrick, Brian. *The Duffer's Guide to Bogey Golf.* Englewood Cliffs, NJ: Prentice-Hall, Inc., 1973.

Trevino, Lee. *Groove Your Swing My Way.* New York: Atheneum/Smi, 1976.

Trevino, Lee. *Putt for Dough* (videotape). Los Angeles: Paramount Pictures Corp, 1989. (Directed and produced by Don R. Schwab.)

United States Golf Association. *Golf Rules in Pictures.* New York: Perigee, 1988.

Watson, Tom, with Nick Seitz. *Getting Up and Down.* New York: Random House, 1983.

Watson, Tom, with Frank Hannigan. *The USGA's Golf Rules in Pictures.* New York: Times Books, 1988.

Webster's Tenth New Collegiate Dictionary. Springfield, MA: Merriam-Webster Inc., 1993.